Lecture Notes
in Business Information Processing   164

T0171849

Jorge E. Hernández   Shaofeng Liu
Boris Delibašić   Pascale Zaraté
Fátima Dargam   Rita Ribeiro (Eds.)

Decision Support Systems II - Recent Developments Applied to DSS Network Environments

Euro Working Group Workshop, EWG-DSS 2012
Liverpool, UK, April 12-13, 2012
and Vilnius, Lithuania, July 8-11, 2012
Revised Selected and Extended Papers

 Springer

Volume Editors

Jorge E. Hernández
University of Liverpool, UK
E-mail: j.e.hernandez@liverpool.ac.uk

Shaofeng Liu
University of Plymouth, UK
E-mail: shaofeng.liu@plymouth.ac.uk

Boris Delibašić
University of Belgrade, Serbia
E-mail: boris.delibasic@fon.bg.ac.rs

Pascale Zaraté
Toulouse 1 Capitole University, France
E-mail: zarate@irit.fr

Fátima Dargam
SimTech Simulation Technology, Graz, Austria
E-mail: f.dargam@simtechnology.com

Rita Ribeiro
UNINOVA–CA3, Lisbon, Portugal
E-mail: rar@uninova.pt

ISSN 1865-1348   e-ISSN 1865-1356
ISBN 978-3-642-41076-5   e-ISBN 978-3-642-41077-2
DOI 10.1007/978-3-642-41077-2
Springer Heidelberg New York Dordrecht London

Library of Congress Control Number: 2013949649

Typesetting: Camera-ready by author, data conversion by Scientific Publishing Services, Chennai, India

Printed on acid-free paper

Springer is part of Springer Science+Business Media (www.springer.com)

Preface

This second edition of post-proceeding publication organized by the main EWG-DSS events in 2012, contains extended and revised versions of a set of selected papers submitted and presented at the EWG-DSS research events held in Liverpool and Vilnius in April and July 2012, respectively. Those events included one workshop and the DSS stream organization in the 2012 EURO conference. Both were supported and sponsored by the Euro Working Group on Decision Support Systems (EWG-DSS) and the Association of European Operational Research Societies (EURO), in cooperation with the Management School University of Liverpool (ULMS), UK, University of Toulouse, the Institut de Research en Informatique de Toulouse (IRIT), France, UNINOVA Computational Intelligence Research Group (CA3), Portugal, School of Management University of Plymouth, UK, SimTech Simulation Technology, Austria, Instituto de Lógica Filosofia e Teoria da Ciência (ILTC), Brazil, and University of Belgrade, Serbia.

The major objective of the EWG-DSS Workshop 2012 in Liverpool and of the DSS Stream at the 25th European Conference on Operational Research in Vilnius was to bring together academics, researchers, practitioners, and enterprises interested in modelling, implementing, and deploying decision support systems for enhancing the decision-making process in different types of environments, considering conceptual as well as applied approaches. Hence, the scientific areas of interest for selected contributions from these two outstanding events were: integrated DSS for global manufacturing, DSS supported by simulation and optimization approaches, centralised and non-centralised decision-making in manufacturing networks, knowledge management and DSS in industries, DSS reference studies, methods, languages and tools to support decision making. This rich variety of themes within the contributions, allowed us to present in this edition a summary of the solutions for the implementation of decision-making process in diverse environments, showing its trends' evolution. In this context, the selected papers are representative of the current relevant research activities in the area of decision support systems such as decision analysis for enterprise systems and non-hierarchical networks, integrated solutions for decision support and knowledge management in distributed environments, decision support systems evaluations and analysis through social networks, e-learning context and their application to real environments.

Both 2012 EWG-DSS events, Liverpool and Vilnius, considered 24 and 9 paper presentations, respectively. From the total of 33 papers, 9 papers were accepted for publication in this edition by considering their content, structure and presentation qualities. This leads to a "full-paper" acceptance ratio of 27%, following the EWG-DSS tradition in preserving a high-quality forum for the next editions of these EWG-DSS events. The post-proceedings' selection and publication considered a triple-blind paper evaluation method: each selected paper was reviewed by at least three internationally known experts from the EWG-DSS Program Committee and externally invited reviewers.

The high quality of these two events in 2012 was aligned with the highly-qualified attendance expectations. In particular, the Liverpool's EWG-DSS work-shop program was enhanced by six keynote lectures, delivered by distinguished guests who are renowned experts in their fields, including:

- Dr. Paul Drake, Head of Marketing and Operations Management Group, Management School, University of Liverpool, UK.
- Prof. Pascale Zaraté, Professeur at Université Toulouse 1 Capitole (UT1C). France.
- Mr. Tony Waller, Lanner Group, UK.
- Dr. Stephen Childe, Senior lecturer at the School of Engineering, Computing and Mathematics, University of Exeter, UK.
- Prof. Peter McBurney. Agents and Intelligent Systems Group of the Depart-ment of Informatics at King's College London, UK.
- Dr. Zenon Michaelides. Management School, University of Liverpool, UK.

Their lectures were very interesting and there was a high level of information exchange for further fruitful cooperation among all participants.

This EWG-DSS Springer LNBIP Edition includes the contributions described in the sequel. "The Development Roadmap of the EWG-DSS Collab-Net Project: A Social Network Perspective of DSS Research Collaboration in Europe", a pa-per that presents the publication network analysis project of the EWG-DSS, authored by Fátima Dargam, Isabelle Linden, Shaofeng Liu, Rita A. Ribeiro, and Pascale Zaraté. "Testing the Seddon Model of Information System Success in an E-Learning Context: Implications for Evaluating DSS," authored by Sean Eom; "The Benefits of SaaS-based Enterprise Systems for SMEs - A Litera-ture Review," a contribution that won the EWG-DSS 2012-Award in Liverpool, authored by Gwendolin Schaefer, Marion Schulze, Yahaya Yusuf and Ahmed Musa. "An operational planning solution for SMEs in collaborative and non-hierarchical networks," authored by Beatriz Andrés, Raul Poler and Jorge E. Hernández. "On the Application of AHP to the Diagnostic of Portuguese SME", authored by Bruno Gonçalo Nunes, João Paulo Costa and Pedro Godinho. "A DSS Solution for Integrated Automated Bidding, Subcontractor Selection and Project Scheduling", authored by Alireza Pakgohar, Stephen J. Childe and David Z. Zhang. "An integrative knowledge management framework to support ERP implementation for improved management decision making in industry", au-thored by Uchitha Jayawickrama, Shaofeng Liu and Melanie Hudson Smith. "A Web-Based Decision Support System using Basis Update on Simplex Type Algo-rithms," authored by Nikolaos Ploskas, Nikolaos Samaras, Jason Papathanasiou, and the contribution entitled "Decision Analysis in Magnox Limited: Develop-ments in Techniques and Stakeholder Engagement Processes," authored by Si-mon Turner and Stephen Wilmott.

We would like to take this opportunity to express our gratitude to all those who contributed to the 2012 EWG-DSS research events in Liverpool and Vilnius, including authors, reviewers, Program Committees and institutional sponsorships. Finally, we hope you will find all the addressed contents useful and interesting to cope with many of the decision support systems challenges in terms of research and practice activities to be referenced in the future when addressing any of the research areas previously mentioned.

August 2013

Jorge E. Hernández
Shaofeng Liu
Boris Delibašić
Pascale Zaraté
Fátima Dargam
Rita Ribeiro

EURO Working Group on Decision Support Systems

The EWG-DSS is a Working Group on Decision Support Systems within EURO, the Association of the European Operational Research Societies. The main purpose of the EWG-DSS is to establish a platform for encouraging state-of-the-art high quality research and collaboration work within the DSS community. Other aims of the EWG-DSS are to:

- Encourage the exchange of information among practitioners, end-users, and researchers in the area of decision systems.
- Enforce the networking among the DSS communities available and facilitate activities that are essential for the start-up of international cooperation research and projects.
- Facilitate professional academic and industrial opportunities for its members.
- Favor the development of innovative models, methods and tools in the field decision support and related areas.
- Actively promote the interest on Decision Systems in the scientific community by organizing dedicated workshops, seminars, mini-conferences, and conference streams in major conferences, as well as editing special and contributed issues in relevant scientific journals.

The EWG-DSS was founded with 24 members, during the EURO Summer Institute on DSS that took place at Madeira, Portugal, in May 1989, organized by two well-known academics of the OR Community: Jean-Pierre Brans and José Paixão. The EWG-DSS group has substantially grown over the years. Currently, we count 230 registered multi-national members.

Through the years, much collaboration between the group members generated valuable contributions to the DSS field, which resulted in many journal publications. Since its creation, the EWG-DSS has held annual meetings in various European countries, and has taken active part in the EURO conferences on decision-making related subjects.

The EWG-DSS coordination board is composed by: Pascale Zaraté (France), Fátima Dargam (Austria), Rita Ribeiro (Portugal), Jorge E. Hernández (UK), Boris Delibašić (Serbia), and Shaofeng Liu (UK).

Organization

Conference Chairs

Fátima Dargam	SimTech Simulation Technology, Austria
Pascale Zaraté	IRIT / Toulouse University, France
Rita Ribeiro	UNINOVA – CA3 Portugal
Jorge E. Hernández	University of Liverpool, UK
Shaofeng Liu	University of Plymouth, UK
Boris Delibašić	University of Belgrade, Serbia

Program Committee

Alex Brodsky	George Mason University, USA
Ana Respício	University of Lisbon, Portugal
Andrew C. Lyons	ULMS – University of Liverpool, UK
Antonio Rodrigues	University of Lisbon, Portugal
Boris Delibašić	University of Belgrade, Serbia
Csaba Csaki	University College Cork, Ireland
Dragana Becejski-Vujaklija	University of Belgrade, Serbia
Fátima Dargam	SimTech Simulation Technology / ILTC, Austria
Frédreric Adam	University College Cork, Ireland
Hossam Ismail	ULMS – University of Liverpool, UK
Jason Papathanasiou	University of Macedonia, Greece
João Lourenço	IST, Technical University of Lisbon, Portugal
João Paulo Costa	University of Coimbra, Portugal
Jorge Freire de Souza	Engineering University of Porto, Portugal
Jorge Pinho de Sousa	Engineering University of Porto, Portugal
Jorge Hernández	ULMS – University of Liverpool, UK
José Maria Moreno	Zaragoza University, Spain
Marko Bohanec Jozef	Stefan Institute, Ljubljana, Slovenia
Pascale Zaraté	IRIT / Toulouse University, France
Peter Keenan	BS / University College Dublin, Ireland
Philip Powel	Birkbeck, University of London, UK
Raul Rodriguez	Universidad Politecnica de Valencia, Spain
Raul Poler	Universidad Politecnica de Valencia, Spain
Rahul Savani	DCS – University of Liverpool, UK
Rita Ribeiro	UNINOVA – CA3, Portugal
Rudolf Vetschera	University of Vienna, Austria
Sean Eom	Southeast Missouri State University, USA
Shaofeng Liu	University of Plymouth, UK

Organizing Committee

EWG-DSS

Fátima Dargam	SimTech Simulation Technology, Austria
Pascale Zaraté	IRIT / Toulouse University, France
Rita Ribeiro	UNINOVA – CA3, Portugal
Jorge Hernández	University of Liverpool, UK
Shaofeng Liu	University of Plymouth, UK
Boris Delibašić	University of Belgrade, Serbia

Liverpool – 2012 EWG-DSS Workshop

Jorge Hernández	University of Liverpool Management School, UK
Katie Neary	University of Liverpool Management School, UK
Artemis Mermigki	University of Liverpool Management School, UK

Vilnius – DSS Stream at 25th European Conference on Operational Research

Fátima Dargam	SimTech Simulation Technology, Austria
Pascale Zaraté	IRIT / Toulouse University, France
Shaofeng Liu	University of Plymouth, UK

Technical Sponsors

Working Group on Decision Support Systems
(http://ewgdss.wordpress.com/)

Association of European Operational Research Societies
(www.euro-online.org)

Organizational Co-sponsors

Management School, University of Liverpool, UK
(http://www.liv.ac.uk/management/)

University of Toulouse, France

(http://www.univ-tlse1.fr/)

IRIT Institut de Research en Informatique de Toulouse, France (http://www.irit.fr/)

UNINOVA - CA3 - Computational Intelligence Research Group (www.uninova.pt/ca3/)

School of Management, University of Plymouth, UK
(http://www.plymouth.ac.uk/)

SimTech Simulation Technology, Austria
(http://www.SimTechnology.com)
ILTC - Instituto de Lógica Filosofia e Teoria da Ciência, RJ, Brazil (http://www.iltc.br)

University of Belgrade, Serbia
(http://www.bg.ac.rs/eng/uni/university.php)

Table of Contents

The Development Roadmap of the EWG-DSS Collab-Net Project: A Social Network Perspective of DSS Research Collaboration in Europe

Fátima Dargam[1,*], Isabelle Linden[2], Shaofeng Liu[3],
Rita A. Ribeiro[4], and Pascale Zaraté[5]

[1] SimTech Simulation Technology, Austria
f.dargam@simtechnology.com
[2] University of Namur, Belgium
isabelle.linden@unamur.be
[3] University of Plymouth, UK
shaofeng.liu@plymouth.ac.uk
[4] UNINOVA – CA3, Portugal
rar@uninova.pt
[5] IRIT / University of Toulouse, France
pascale.zarate@ut-capitole.fr

Abstract. It is well-known that social network analysis has been playing an increasingly important role in evaluating scientific research collaboration within publication databases. This paper presents the development roadmap of the EWG-DSS Collab-Net Project of the EURO Working Group on Decision Support Systems. The current project serves as a means for a social network perspective of research collaboration within the Decision Support Systems community in Europe. The major key variable used for the network analysis is co-authorship. The network was designed to show the collaboration dynamics among the researchers, members of the EWG-DSS group. Newly in this paper is the specification of the ontology model to be used within the collaboration research network, stating its benefits to the project. The study provides a clear understanding of the community's strengths, in terms of key players, strong links and well researched topic areas; as well as weaknesses such as weak links and isolated researchers. The main goal of the project's network analysis is to allow researchers to seek opportunities for future collaboration within the DSS communities. Results achieved so far are briefly described within the paper.

Keywords: Social Network Analysis, EWG-DSS, Scientific Research Collaboration, Co-authorship, Ontology Model, Project EWG-DSS-Collab-Net.

1 Introduction

Social network analysis produces an alternative view, where emphasis is not strongly given to the attributes of discrete units of analysis, but rather to their relationships and

---

[*] Fátima Dargam also collaborates as a senior researcher at ILTC Institute of Logic and Theory of Science (www.iltc.br) in Rio de Janeiro, Brazil.

J.E. Hernández et al. (Eds.): EWG-DSS 2012, LNBIP 164, pp. 1–18, 2013.
© Springer-Verlag Berlin Heidelberg 2013

ties with other actors within the network. It focuses on how the structure of ties affects individual nodes, which can represent persons, organizations, states and their relationships. Social network analysis can provide insights into both interaction patterns and network statistics [1]. Its power mainly stems from its difference from traditional social scientific studies [2-3].

Collaboration and affiliation networks are specific types of social networks. An affiliation network can be seen as a network of individuals connected by common membership in groups of some sort, such as clubs, teams, or organisations [4]. Data on affiliation networks tend to be more reliable than those on other social networks, since membership of a group can often be precisely determined as a relationship. Similarly, scientific collaboration networks are typical social networks with vertices representing scientists and edges representing collaborations among them [5]. Tangible and well-documented forms of collaboration among scientists include co-authorship and co-citation [4, 6].

Over the years, the EURO Working Group on Decision Support Systems (EWG-DSS) of the Association of the European Operational Research Societies has identified the need to better structure its collaboration dynamics in order to provide its members with better chances for joint research work. Since its foundation in 1989, a number of well-qualified research co-operations within group members have been established, which have generated valuable contributions to the DSS field such as journal publications. More recently, those publications have been extensively encouraged with the organisation of the EWG-DSS annual research events. Evidences of those editions can be found in [7-15]. Since 2008, the EWG-DSS Co-ordination Board have been undertaking a network analysis project, defining a publication co-authorship network structure, which has been subject of further enhancements and updates up to date.

This paper describes the specifications and versions of the EWG-DSS Collaboration Network Project (EWG-DSS-Collab-Net), showing its new trends and advances. It is organised into six sections. The following section reviews the related work in scientific collaboration and co-authorship networks. Section 3 introduces the EWG-DSS and its project EWG-DSS-Collab-Net (versions 1 and 2). Section 4 describes the ontology model specified for the project. Section 5 briefly presents the new trends and proposals of the current developments of the EWG-DSS collaboration network. Section 6 concludes the work with future work.

2   Research Collaboration and Co-authorship

Many different forms of collaboration have been explored in scientific communities, such as through visiting scholars, co-editorialship, joint PhD supervision, collaborative research projects, and joint writing. In the most formal way, the collaboration can be tangibly documented such as via joint publications and shared patents. At other times, collaboration may be in a less formal way such as interaction at conferences, workshops, seminars, and feedback from reviewers and editors.

Existing work in social network analysis has investigated collaboration within affiliation networks in a wide range of disciplines, using formal and informal forms of collaboration. Some of the collaboration and co-authorship analysis literature focused on scientific fields including biology [16], computer science [5], geography [1], management and organisational studies [16-17], mathematics [18], physics [19], research and development [20], and tourism and hospitality management [21]. A few publications have discussed inter-disciplinary collaboration networks [22-23]. The collaboration has been reported at various levels, including individual level [18], national level [20, 22, 24], and international level [22].

Two tangible and well-documented methods used for the study of research collaboration are co-authorship and co-citation analysis. In co-citation networks, links between researchers are established through authors' references to each other's publications [18]. Co-authorship networks are quite distinctive, in the sense that the nodes of the networks are authors rather than papers [5], [22-23]. Therefore it is perceived that the co-citation networks depict the structure of knowledge in the scientific community, whereas co-authorship networks depict a scientific society, providing an opportunity to identify and measure the extent of social influence and interaction. While co-citation analysis might help identify the central and important scientific papers, co-authorship analysis can help identify the most influential scientists in the community [21], further help facilitate the knowledge flow within the network (knowledge diffuse through the key nodes and shortest paths), assess the resilience of the network (preventing attack to weakly connected nodes) and formulate strategies for the community growth (using the key players to influence others to join in the society). On the above basis, this paper adopted co-authorship analysis for the study of DSS research collaboration in Europe, specifically using the co-authorship as the primary indicator of relationship between the researchers of the EWG-DSS network.

3   The EWG-DSS and Project EWG-DSS-Collab-Net

The primary aim of EWG-DSS is to provide a platform for encouraging state-of-the-art high quality research and collaboration work within the DSS community [51]. Other aims include to encourage the exchange of information and knowledge among DSS researchers; facilitate international cooperation; promote the interest on DSS in the scientific community by organizing dedicated workshops, seminars, mini-conferences, etc.; disseminate high quality research by editing special and contributed issues in relevant scientific journals; enforce networking among its members and international DSS communities; and inspire the development of innovative models, methods and tools in the DSS field and related areas.

Since its creation, the EWG-DSS has held annual Meetings in various European countries, and has taken active part in the EURO Conferences on decision-making related subjects. The number of EWG-DSS members has substantially grown along the years. By the end of 2012, it counted with 163 registered members and more than 150 members in its Linked-In Group of Interest. So far, we have achieved 190 registered memberships.

Since 2008 the EWG-DSS Coordination Board has been conducting a study about research interests of the group members, with the intention to draw a knowledge map on Decision Support Systems within its community. The EWG-DSS Collaboration Research Network (EWG-DSS Collab-Net) has then started and has been continuously enhanced. Some of the advances of the project were published in [25-31]. In this paper, we revisit the project work cited above, with a focus on social-academic network to provide an overall picture of the project. Newly presented in this paper is the specification of the project's Ontology Data Structure Model. In the following subsections, we give more details of the EWG-DSS Collab-Net project in its versions 1 and 2.

Initial Empirical Method and Building Methodology

For the acquisition of the academic production used in the first developed network of the EWG-DSS Collab-Net [25, 28], all the members of the DSS group were requested by the coordination board to submit relevant information, concerning their publications since 1989, stating for each of them the main areas of research, apart from the co-authorship and edition details. As a result, 70 members replied with their feedback. From the information received, a total of 1350 publications were taken into consideration for a case-study. Only international publications of the EWG-DSS members were considered. Outside collaborators of the publications, not members of the EWG-DSS, were not included in the initial network.

To construct and analyse the social academic network, five main steps were carried out: 1. acquisition process - collecting input data in a matrix, which could relate authors and their papers, as well as the papers classified into topics; 2. extraction process - creating the input files with nodes and labels to enable them to be manipulated by the network tools PAJEK [32-35] and NWB [36]; 3. transformation process - using Jaccard similarity measure [37], we constructed a set of weighted networks by combining matrices including authors, publications and research topics; 4. weighted network graphical analysis - using PAJEK and NBW graphical tools, we analyzed the main characteristics of the EWG-DSS group; and 5. network statistics - using PAJEK and NBW statistical tools, the main aspects of the academic network were depicted. For more details of the study undertaken for the initial implementation of the EWG-DSS network, the readers should refer to the work published in [25-28] and [31].

EWG-DSS-Collab-Net V.1

The EWG-DSS-Collab-Net in its version V.1 counted with 70 authors' input data of 1350 publications, covering the period from 1989 to 2008, of which 34 topics of research areas were extracted (see Table 1 below). It featured relationships like "author-publication-topic", taking into account one topic per publication for its analysis.

The EWG-DSS Collab-Net V.1 included sub-networks representing relationships among authors, publications, projects and research areas. The relations reflected the collaborations, joint-projects, journal-editions, etc. The initial objective was to detect the research distances among the members of the group; the major and minor areas of research concentration; the interaction in the group; new tendencies and working areas; as well as new opportunities for cooperation.

Table 1. Topics of research extracted from the 1350 publications

#	Research Topic	#	Research Topic
1	Business Models	18	Knowledge Management
2	Collaboration Dynamics	19	Multi-Agent Systems
3	Cooperative Decision Support Systems	20	Multiple Criteria Decision Aiding
4	Decision Analysis	21	Management Learning and Decision Making
5	Decision Aiding Process	22	Network
6	Data Mining	23	Operations research
7	Decision Support Systems	24	Preference analysis
8	Evaluation	25	Performance Evaluation
9	E-Business	26	Preference Modelling
10	Entreprise resource Planning	27	Production Planning and Scheduling
11	Expert Systems	28	Supply Chain Management
12	Economic Theory	29	Sustainable Development
13	Fuzzy Sets	30	Social Networks
14	Group Decision and Negotiation	31	Simulation Systems
15	Information Retrieval	32	Systems Software Evaluation and Selection
16	Information Systems	33	Virtual Communities
17	Information and Telecommunication Technology	34	Context

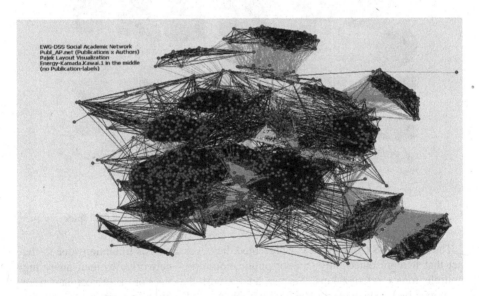

Fig. 1. EWG-DSS-Collab-Net V.1 - Publication collaboration among authors

To accomplish those goals, we created the initial matrices needed to represent the relationships and we used matrix multiplication process to combine the information of both Boolean matrices including the authors and their publications and their respective research topics, via their input networks. For the graphical representation and analysis of the network, we chose the network frameworks PAJEK [32] and NWB [36]. The PAJEK framework is from design dedicated to large network analysis, whereas the NWB Network Workbench is a framework for pre-processing, modelling and analysing small networks. Both of them are MS-Windows-based programs designed for network analysis and visualization. Figure 1 illustrates the analysis of the network, concerning the output network "Publications x Authors". In Figure 2, we can identify the clusters of publications, relative to the topics listed in Table 1. In this visualization of the "Publications x Topics" network, it is clearly seen that almost 25% of the topics, relative to 8 larger sub-nets, concentrate the great majority of papers published among the EWG-DSS group members. More details about the EWG-DSS-Collab-Net V.1 implementation can be found in [27] and [28].

Visualizations of single players, egonet visualizations, relating authors and research topics, were also analysed in version 1. In Figure 3 below, we can observe a *Radial Graph* visualization of the network "Authors x Topics", where it is possible to verify how the 70 authors are interconnected to each other with relation to their main topics of research, taking two arbitrarily authors as central nodes (A9 and A65). In this particular case, nodes A9 and A65 are bridging two different areas of research within the network. It is relevant to notice that the darker connections, represented in the foreground, express the stronger connections among the authors and the nodes in focus.

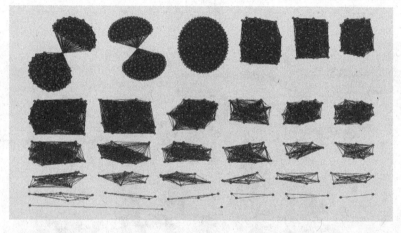

Fig. 2. EWG-DSS-Collab-Net V.1 - Publications distributed among the topics

The EWG-DSS Collab-Net V.1 presented, however, analysis limitations due to the fact that it represented only "author-publication-topic" networks, without analysing multiple topics relationships. Further analysis of the Version 1 project has been developed by Dardenne from University of Namur in Belgium in cooperation with the EWG-DSS [38]. In [38], the usual measures on the graph and on its nodes, as well as the measures of centrality (degree centrality; betweenness centrality; eigenvector centrality) and applications of communities detection methods were used to respond to issues concerning the identification of the authors that were the most collaborative; the creation of sub-communities among the several connected components; and the existence of concentrations of authors within the network. To implement the network, the tool NodeXL was used [38]. The main goal of that study was to exploit and enhance EWG-DSS Collab-Net Version 1 in order to prepare it for Version 2 [30-31].

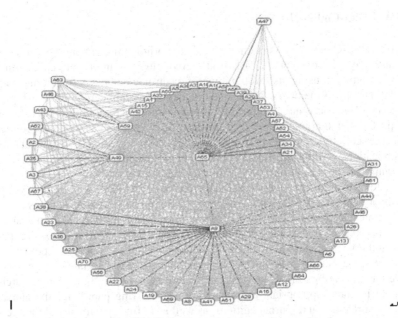

Fig. 3. EWG-DSS-Collab-Net V.1 – Egonet relating authors and topics

Dardenne's analysis has brought us one step closer to reaching our main goals. Interesting observations of the community relations could be taken from the work in [38], via its centrality analysis. For instance, the case of people with a more modest centrality degree, having a high betweeness centrality was observed. They are key players of the DSS community, acting as bridges between non isolated clusters [30, 38]. Dardenne has also introduced in his study the relation "Authors x Authors", in which authors are linked by their common publications. This way, the represented network identified extra 782 authors out of the original 70 authors, members of the EWG-DSS, who contributed to the original 1350 publications.

In conclusion, the collaboration relationships in EWG-DSS Collab-Net V.1 have shown how the researchers relate to each other in terms of topics of research; what the most relevant topics of research are; and the relevant statistical data concerning the publications. The output of this version devised an academic-social network analysis, which identified the collaboration relationship that exists among the group members, as well as how the group's dynamics has evolved since its foundation in 1989. The metrics of the network graphical representations helped us to build up a consistent basis for analyzing the network graphs that were generated via the input data available. Weak connections among researchers were identified. However, based on the study conducted by Granovetter in social networks [39], we have attributed great potential for the weak connections of the EWG-DSS network to be able to develop into strong ones. From [39], we know that information is far more likely to be "diffused" through weaker ties, than through already strong connections. In the particular case of the EWG-DSS network, also absent connections from isolated publications should be considered. They should be encouraged to become "weak ties", in order to gain more relevance within the network and consequently also within the group. This issue was little exploited in Version 1 and is addressed in the developments of EWG-DSS Collab-Net Version 2.

EWG-DSS-Collab-Net V.2

EWG-DSS-Collab-Net Version 2 extends the original implementation of Version 1 in many ways. It considers: 1) a hybrid methodology of input data collection (manual and automatic), using also web mining of electronic databases to automatically detect relationships of members; 2) a refined model of the publication relationship structure, taking into account "author-title-journal/conference-multiple keywords-multiple topics"; 3) an ontology-based data structure model; as well as 4) a more refined model of the collaboration relationship structure, which includes workshop/conference publications, informal work meetings, event co-organisations, scientific committees/boards, book/journal editorials, etc.

Along with social network analysis statistics, EWG-DSS-Collab-Net V.2 performs collaboration trend analysis, showing co-authorships and co-citations to further illustrate the dynamics of EWG-DSS publications overtime. The analysis features, among other characteristics, (a) the number and percentage of multi-author papers and co-authors in comparison with single-author papers; (b) number and percentage of co-citations; (c) identification of publications that are closely related to a given topic, as well as the authors involved. This last feature helps specially to find researchers who could be more appropriate to collaborate in reviewing papers for the annual EWG-DSS workshops and journal editions, as well as to find specifically skilled researchers among the members of the group to collaborate on projects. Most of all, the extended analysis of EWG-DSS Collab-Net V.2 plans to promote continued new research and collaboration among the academic members of the group and to attract new members for further fruitful collaboration.

In [28], it is shown how co-authorship has been explored as the key indicator for the collaboration among European DSS researchers. The research report [31] describes the development and analysis of the collaboration network V.2, in order to obtain a social network perspective on the DSS research collaboration across Europe, with the main purpose to improve the data objectivity and analysis accuracy to avoid the claimed shortcomings of social network analysis being poor statistical accuracy and intrinsic subjectivity. In Figure 4 we illustrate the blocks specification of the EWG-DSS-Collab-Net V.2 for its implementation, showing where the ontology model will be concentrated.

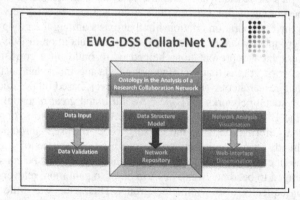

Fig. 4. EWG-DSS-Collab-Net V.2 – Implementation Specification

The data input for EWG-DSS Collab-Net V.2, conceives a hybrid methodology of input data collection (manual and automatic), including web mining of publications electronic databases like: DBLP Computer Science Bibliography; SciVerse Scopus; Google Scholar; Microsoft Academic Search; Private Publications URL; among others. The Data Validation module takes into account the various scripts and crawlers' codes to capture and filter the relevant input information from the chosen input web-environments. It caters for the validation of the publications input data (including knowledge areas, keywords) and authors' information, as well as for its normalization. Figure 5 illustrates how the Data Validation operates within EWG-DSS-Collab-Net V.2 Data Input Module.

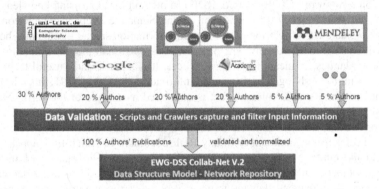

Fig. 5. EWG-DSS-Collab-Net V.2 – Data Input Module / Data Validation

Building upon the development of Version 1, EWG-DSS-Collab-Net V.2 tackles the following issues: appropriate data structure; ontology models to classify and interpret the data; selection of ready-to-use ontologies to be adopted, like bibo (Bibliographic Ontology Specification), foaf (FOAF Vocabulary Specification), owl (OWL Web Ontology Language) and skos (SKOS Core Vocabulary Specification); as well as the selection and implementation of appropriate network structures; social network environments; and analysis metrics for the network.

4   Ontology Model

The EWG-DSS-Collab-Net V.2 considers a publication relationship structured model, with authors-publications and multiple keywords and topics. The social network analysis shows co-authorships and co-citations overtime. In order to refine the identification of publications that are closely related to a given topic, an ontology model is specified [40]. This way, a common vocabulary of classifications relative to the main areas of the publications can be defined and matched with the existing publications key-words. The concern of applying ontology models to improve knowledge management and decision-making, was already introduced in [41], in which some of the inherent advantages were elicited.

An ontology is an explicit specification of a conceptualization. An ontology model can be described by defining its set of representational terms within a particular formal way. For knowledge-based systems, what "exists" is exactly that which can be represented: the *Universe of Discourse*. In an ontology, definitions associate the names of entities in the universe of discourse *(e.g., classes, relations, functions, or other objects)* with human-readable text describing what the names are meant to denote, and formal axioms that constrain the interpretation and well-formed use of those terms [43].

The EWG-DSS Collab-Net Ontology Model

In order to represent the EWG-DSS-Collab-Net V.2 Data Structure Model, the Resource Description Framework (RDF) is used. RDF is a method for expressing knowledge in a decentralized world and is the foundation of the Semantic Web, in which computer applications make use of distributed, structured information spread throughout the Web [49], [50]. RDF decomposes any type of knowledge into small pieces, with some rules about the semantics, or meaning, of those pieces. It is a particularly useful technology when you want to mesh together distributed information, including URL links. RDF can be defined in three simple rules: A fact is expressed as a triple of the form (*Subject, Predicate, Object*). It's like an English sentence. Subjects, predicates, and objects are names for entities, whether concrete or abstract, in the real world. Names are either 1) global and refer to the same entity in any RDF document in which they appear, or 2) local, and the entity it refers to cannot be directly referred to outside of the RDF document. Objects can also be text values, called literal values. The subject denotes the resource, and the predicate denotes traits or aspects of the resource and expresses a relationship between the subject and the object. What makes RDF suited for distributed knowledge is that its applications can put together RDF files posted by different people around the Internet and easily learn from them new things that no single document asserted. It does this in two ways, first by linking documents together by the common vocabularies they use, and second by allowing any document to use any vocabulary. This flexibility is fairly unique to RDF. There are two complementary ways of looking at RDF information. The first is as a set of statements, each one representing a fact. The second way is as a graph, which is basically a network. Graphs consist of nodes interconnected by edges. In RDF, the nodes are names (not actual entities) and the edges are statements (see Figure 6).

The EWG-DSS Collab-Net Data Structure Model represented by RDF counts with the power of an ontology model in order to classify and interpret the data. For some specific tasks, like bibliography handling; vocabulary specification; memberships associations; thesauri, taxonomies and classification schemes, there are available solutions via the use ready-to-use ontologies. Based on the well-known performance of the available ontologies [44, 45, 46, 47, 48], the following ontologies are considered in the Ontology Model of our project:

- BIBO (Bibliographic Ontology) (*www.biblioontology.com*);
- FOAF ("Friend of a Friend" Ontology) (*http://www.foaf-project.org/*);
- OWL (OWL Web Ontology Language) (http://www.w3.org/TR/owl-ref/); and
- SKOS (Simple Knowledge Organization System); &
- SKOS Core *(*http://www.w3.org/TR/swbp-skos-core-guide).

BIBO is a Bibliographic Ontology [44] that describes bibliographic things on the Semantic Web in RDF. It is mainly used as a citation ontology and as a document classification ontology. It can also be used as a common ground for converting other bibliographic data sources. It provides main concepts and properties for describing citations and bibliographic references (i.e. quotes, books, articles, etc) on the Semantic Web. BIBO includes 189 Resources, namely: 69 Classes {AcademicArticle; AudioDocument; Book; Journal; ...}; 52 Object Properties {authorList; citedBy; editor; reviewOf; ...}; 54 Data Properties {abstract; chapter; edition; identifier; ...}; and 14 Individuals {degrees/ms; degrees/phd; status/accepted; status/legal...}.

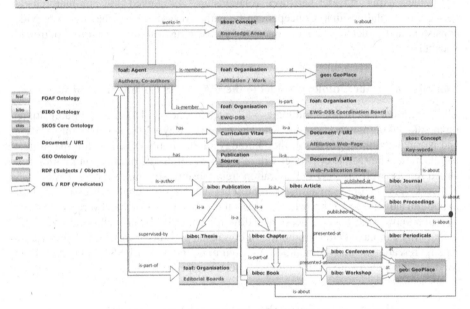

Fig. 6. EWG-DSS-Collab-Net V.2 – Data Model with Ontology Model

The FOAF ontology ("Friend of a Friend") [45] is originated from a Semantic Web project described as a "practical experiment" in the application of RDF (Resource Description Framework) Data Model and Semantic Web technologies to social networking. FOAF is a project devoted to linking people and information using the Web. It integrates three kinds of network: social networks of human collaboration, friendship and association; representational networks that describe a simplified view of a cartoon universe in factual terms; and information networks that use web-based linking to share independently published descriptions of this inter-connected world. FOAF includes Classes like: | Agent | Document | Group | OnlineAccount | Organization | Person | Project | etc; and Properties like: | account | accountName | age | currentProject | familyName | gender | member, among others.

OWL is a Web Ontology Language [46]. The OWL is intended to provide a language that can be used to describe the classes and relations between them that are inherent in Web documents and applications. It is a semantic markup language for publishing and sharing ontologies on the World Wide Web.

SKOS - Simple Knowledge Organization System [47], is a formal language and schema designed to represent such structured information domains as thesauri, classification schemes, taxonomies, subject-heading systems, controlled vocabularies, etc. Using SKOS, concepts can be: identified, labeled in natural languages, assigned notations, documented; linked to other concepts and organized into informal hierarchies and association networks; aggregated into concept schemes; grouped into labeled and/or ordered collections, and mapped to concepts in other schemes. SKOS Core [48] defines the classes and properties based on a concept-centric view of the vocabulary. Each SKOS concept is defined as an RDF data model resource. Each concept can have RDF properties attached to it. Concepts can be organized in hierarchies using broader-narrower relationships, or linked by non-hierarchical (associative) relationships. Concepts can be gathered in concept schemes, to provide consistent and structured sets of concepts, representing whole or part of a controlled vocabulary.

Contribution of the Ontology Model to the EWG-DSS Collab-Net Project

The Data Model including Ontologies will cater for the validation of the publications input data, taking into account the Knowledge areas; Keywords; Authors' information and Normalization. In Figure 4, the Ontology Model is illustrated within the project architecture. The Ontology Model will allow us to refine the publication relationship structure, as well as the collaboration relationship structure of the EWG-DSS Network. As a direct benefit, it represents better structured processes to take maximum advantage of knowledge. Also the ontologies can be leveraged to help improve knowledge management and allow for better decisions. This way, the DSS community can have better promotion of continued and further research collaboration among researchers and co-authors. In Figure 6, the EWG-DSS Collab-Net Data Model is illustrated with the Ontology Model's perspective.

5   Considerations about the Network Development

Previous pieces of work have addressed the social network of the EWG-DSS as a snapshot drawn on the basis of a set of publications [25-31]. The table below (Table 2) shows the development impacts, concerning data input and network analysis, of the existing versions of the EWG-DSS Collab-Net Project.

In the current developments of the EWG-DSS Collab-Net Version 2 and further, the social network is addressed in a new perspective: one which emphasizes the evolution of the DSS community in different aspects. This stage considers all the participants involved with the EWG-DSS organised research events, as well as all the authors and co-authors involved in the related publications. Also the topics of the papers and their research areas will be considered as other aspects of the evolution. On the basis of the author-defined key words, the study exploits existing clusters of publications, the temporal evolution of popular topics, the topic-related sub-group in EWG-DSS and their respective evolution.

Table 2. Development Roadmap of the EWG-DSS Collab-Net Project

EWG-DSS Collab-Net		Version 1 [27,28,29]	Version 1' [38]	Version 2 [30, 31, 40]	Future Versions
Development & Impacts	Data Input and Network Analysis	Manual Data Input. 70 Authors; 1350 Publications; 34 Topics. Author-Publication-Topic Relation (considering only 1 Topic per Paper). Co-authorship Analysis. 3 Networks analysed: Publications x Authors; Publiocations x Topics; Authors x Topics. Identification of Main Areas of Publications and Collaborations among Researchers.	New Analysis via different Centrality Measures. Relation Authors x Authors of common publications. Embedding of the Cooperating Authors (not members of the EWG-DSS) Enlargement of the Authors scope from 70 authors to 782. Identification & Analysis of Sub-Communities of Research Collaboration. Evaluation of new Network Analysis Frameworks.	Conceptual Model for Hybrid Data Collection, including automatic data input via several online publications analysis databases. Ontology-based Data Structure Model. Analysis with Multiple Keywords & Topics per Publication and Conferences & Editions. Co-authorship and Co-citations Analysis. Exploitation of suitable Data Structure and Network Analysis Frameworks.	Implementation & Improvement of the Automatic Collection of Data Input via online citation-databases. Temporal Evolution Analysis, considering co-authorships and co-participation relations. Deployment of a Web-based Version of the Collab-Net Publication Network to be used of the DSS Communities.

The evolution of the so-built network will be mainly observed with regard to its researchers and their relationships (co-author and co-participation), via various relevant density metrics. This proposal will investigate the use of dynamic network analysis tools, in order to better observe and analyse the evolution of the DSS community within a European and international perspective. From the brief description of the current trends and developments of the EWG-DSS collaboration network, it becomes clear that the growing perspective of the EWG-DSS Collab-Net has already assured its landmark as a useful tool for the EWG-DSS members and as an important reference for the European DSS Community as whole.

6   Conclusions

In this paper we revisited the developments of the research collaboration network for the EURO Working Group on DSS, EWG-DSS Collab-Net Project, Versions 1 and 2, stating its objectives, achievements, limitations and current status. Some details of the EWG-DSS Collab-Net V.2 data model structure were newly presented here, including the dedicated ontology model. We strongly believe that the project EWG-DSS Collab-Net is on the right way for providing the DSS community in Europe with more accurate and up-to-date information about research projects and co-authorships, leading to much better future collaboration opportunities.

In terms of future work, there are a few development steps that still need implementation refinements and will be focus of our attention in the future. Namely: inclusion of missing input data (up to the current point in time); Encouragement for the isolated nodes of absent connections to become, at a first stage, nodes of "weak connections" within the net; reduction / elimination of the isolated nodes; deployment of a web-based version of the EWG-DSS Collab-Net project for the use of the European DSS community; augmentation of the EWG-DSS community via the association of the external collaborators (co-authors) present in the network.

To proceed with the planned and pending developments, the EWG-DSS Coordination Board needs the support of all researchers within the group and the DSS Community, via their participation in submitting their data / research production in joint-work, etc; as well as their constructive feedback and help as development force.

Acknowledgements. The authors are very grateful to the constructive comments and recommendations of the referees, which contributed to significant improvements on this publication. This work would not be possible without the cooperation of the EWG-DSS members, who provided the input data for the Collab-Net Project. Special thanks go to all involved DSS researchers in this project, and also to all the technical support received by group members in previous developments, especially the ones published in [16, 31, 38, 40].

References

1. Sun, S., Manson, S.: Social network analysis of the academic GIScience community. The Professional Geographer 63(1), 18–33 (2011)
2. Newman, M.E.J.: The structure and function of complex networks. SIAM Review 45(2), 167–256 (2003)
3. Freeman, F.: Visualizing social networks. Journal of Social Structure 1(1) (2000)
4. Newman, M.E.J.: Scientific collaboration networks. II. Shortest paths, weighted networks, and centrality. Physical Review E 64, 016132 (2001)

5. Shi, Q., Xu, B., Xu, X., Xiao, Y., Wang, W., Wang, H.: Diversity of social ties in scientific collaboration networks. Physica A 390, 4627–4635 (2011)
6. Newman, M.E.J.: Scientific collaboration networks. I. Network construction and fundamental result. Physical Review E 64, 016131 (2001)
7. Dargam, F., Delibasic, B., Hernandez, J., Liu, S., Ribeiro, R., Zarate, P.: Editorial on Decision Systems. In: Proceedings of the EWG-DSS London 2011 Workshop, London, UK, IRIT Research Report: RR–2011-14—FR. Université Paul Sabatier (June 2011)
8. Dargam, F., Delibasic, B., Hernandez, J., Liu, S., Ribeiro, R., Zarate, P.: Editorial on Policy Analytics and Collaborative Decision Making. In: Proceedings of the EWG-DSS / DASIG Joint-Workshop, IRIT, Research Report IRIT/RR–2011-21-FR, Université Paul Sabatier (November-December 2011)
9. Hernández, J.E., Zarate, P., Dargam, F., Delibašić, B., Liu, S., Ribeiro, R. (eds.): EWG-DSS 2011. LNBIP, vol. 121. Springer, Heidelberg (2012)
10. Dargam, F., Delibasic, B., Hernandez, J., Liu, S., Ribeiro, R., Zarate, P.: Editorial on Decision Support Systems & Operations Management Trends and Solutions in Industries. In: Proceedings of the EWG-DSS 2012 Liverpool Workshop (April 2012) ISBN: 978-0-9561122-4-8
11. Dargam, F., Delibasic, B., Hernandez, J., Liu, S.: Special Issue on Networking Decision Making and Negotiation (Part 1). International Journal of Decision Support System Technology, IJDSST 4(2) (2012)
12. Dargam, F., Delibasic, B., Hernandez, J., Liu, S.: Special Issue on Networking Decision Making and Negotiation (Part 2). International Journal of Decision Support System Technology, IJDSST 4(3) (2012)
13. Papathanasiou, J., Liu, S., Zaraté, P.: Special Issue on Collaborative Decision Support Systems. The International Journal of Information and Decision Sciences, IJIDS (2012)
14. Ribeiro, R.A., Moreira, A.M., Broek, P.V.D., Pimentel, A.: Hybrid Assessment Method for Software Engineering Decisions. Decision Support Systems 51, 208–219 (2011)
15. Hernández, J.E., Mula, J., Poler, R., Pavón, J.: A multi-agent negotiation based model to support the collaborative supply chain planning process. Studies in Informatics and Control 20(1), 43–54 (2011)
16. Katerndahl, D.: Evolution of the research collaboration network in a productive department. Journal of Evaluation in Clinical Practice 18, 195–201 (2012)
17. Acedo, F.J., Barroso, C., Casanueva, C., Galan, J.L.: Co-authorship in management and organisational studies: an empirical and network analysis. Journal of Management Studies 43(5), 957–968 (2006)
18. Newman, M.E.J.: Co-authorship networks and patterns of scientific collaboration. Proceedings of the National Academy of Science 101(1), 5200–5205 (2004)
19. Barabasi, A.l., Jeong, H., Neda, Z., Ravasz, E., Schubert, A., Vicsek, T.: Evolution of the social network of scientific collaboration. Physica A: Statistical Mechanics and its Applications 311(3-4), 590–614 (2002)
20. Jin, J.H., Park, S.C., Pyon, C.U.: Finding research trend of convergence technology based on Korean R&D network. Expert Systems with Applications 38, 15159–15171 (2011)
21. Racherla, P., Hu, C.: A social network perspective of tourism research collaborations. Annals of Tourism Research: a Social Sciences Journal 37(4) (2010)
22. Yin, L., Kretschmer, H., Hanneman, R.A., Liu, Z.: Connection and stratification in research collaboration: an analysis of the COLLNET network. Information Processing and Management 42, 1599–1613 (2006)
23. Perc, M.: Growth and structure of Slovenia's scientific collaboration network. Journal of Informatics 4, 475–482 (2010)

24. Xu, X., Yang, L., Liu, F.: Structure of the cross-talk collaboration network of China. Physica A 376, 738–746 (2007)
25. Dargam, F., Ribeiro, R., Zaraté, P.: A Collaboration Network for the EURO Working Group on DSS. In: ISMICK 2008, International Symposium on the Management of Industrial and Corporate Knowledge, Niteroi, Rio de Janeiro, November 3-5 (2008)
26. Dargam, F., Ribeiro, R., Zaraté, P.: Towards a collaboration network for the EURO Working Group on DSS (Advances of the Project). In: Proceedings of the 23rd European Conference on Operational Research, EURO XXIII, Bonn (July 2009)
27. Dargam, F., Ribeiro, R., Zaraté, P.: How does the EURO Working Group on DSS interact? A social academic network analysis 1998-2008. In: Proceedings of the 24th European Conference on Operational Research, EURO XXIV, Lisbon (July 2010)
28. Bouaziz, R., Simas, T., Dargam, F., Ribeiro, R., Zaraté, P.: A Social-Academic Network Analysis of the EURO Working Group on DSS. International Journal of Decision Support Systems Technologies 2(4), 13–36 (2010)
29. Dargam, F., Ribeiro, R., Zaraté, P.: Networking the EWG-DSS: How do we proceed now? (Short Paper). In: Dargam, F., Hernández, J., Liu, S., Ribeiro, R., Zaraté), P. (eds.) Proceedings of the EWG-DSS London-2011 Workshop on Decision Systems, IRIT, Report IRIT/RR–2011-14-FR, Université Paul Sabatier (June 2011)
30. Dardenne, D., Dargam, F., Linden, I., Liu, S., Ribeiro, R., Sun, W., Zaraté, P.: Extending the Analysis of the EURO Working Group on DSS Research Collaboration Network (EWG-DSS Collab-Net V.2). In: Proceedings of the 25th European Conference on Operational Research, EURO XXV (Stream: Decision Support Systems), Vilnius, July 8-11 (2012)
31. Dargam, F., Ribeiro, R., Zarate, P., Liu, S.: A social network perspective of DSS research collaboration in Europe. IRIT, Research Report IRIT/RR–2013-27-FR. Université Paul Sabatier (2013)
32. Mrvar, A., Batagelj, V.: PAJEK - Program for Large Network Analysis (1996-2013), http://pajek.imfm.si/doku.php, http://vlado.fmf.uni-lj.si/pub/networks/pajek/
33. Nooy, W., Mrvar, A., Batagelj, V.: Exploratory Social Network Analysis with Pajek, Revised and Expanded 2nd edn. Structural Analysis in the Social Sciences 34. Cambridge University Press (2011)
34. Mrvar, A., Batagelj, V.: Pajek and Pajek-XXL - Programs for Analysis and Visualization of Very Large Networks: Reference Manual, List of commands with short explanation, version 3.11. Ljubljana (April 2, 2013), http://pajek.imfm.si/lib/exe/fetch.php?media=dl:pajekman.pdf
35. Batagelj, V., Mrvar, A.: Pajek – Analysis and Visualization of Large Networks. In: Junger, M., Mutzel, P. (eds.) Graph Drawing Software. series Mathematics and Visualization, pp. 77–103. Springer, Berlin (2003) ISBN 3-540-00881-0
36. NWB Team, Network Workbench Tool. Indiana University, Northeastern University, and University of Michigan, NWB (2006), http://nwb.slis.indiana.edu
37. Rocha, L.M., Simas, T., Rechtsteiner, A., DiGiacomo, M., Luce, R.: MyLibrary@LANL: Proximity and Semi-metric Networks for a Collaborative and Recommender Web Service. In: Proc. 2005 IEEE/WIC/ ACM International Conference on Web Intelligence (WI 2005), pp. 565–571. IEEE Press (2005)
38. Dardenne, D.: Analyse de réseaux sociaux Propositions pour des études de cas. Master en Ingenieur de Gestion. University of Namur, Faculté des Sciences Economiques, Sociales et de Gestion, 2011-2012 (2012) (in French)

39. Granovetter, M.S.: The Strength of Weak Ties. American Journal of Psychlogy 78(6), 1360–1380 (1973)
40. Branco, A.C.S., Dargam, F., Rademaker, A., Souza, R.: Applying Ontology in the Analysis of a DSS Research Collaboration Network. In: Proceedings of the 25th European Conference on Operational Research, EURO XXV (Stream: Decision Support Systems), Vilnius, July 8-11 (2012)
41. Branco, A.C.S., Dargam, F.C.C.: Ontology bridging Knowledge Management and Decision Making. In: Dargam, F., Delibasic, B., Hernández, J.E., Liu, S., Ribeiro, R., Zaraté, P. (eds.) Proceedings of the EWG-DSS / DASIG Joint-Workshop on Policy Analytics and Collaborative Decision Making, IRIT, Research Report IRIT/RR–2011-21-FR, Université Paul Sabatier (November -December 2011)
42. Hansen, D., Shneiderman, B., Smith, M.: Analyzing Social Media Networks with NodeXL: Insights from a Connected World2. Morgan Kaufmann (2010) ISBN-10: 0123822297
43. Shvaiko, P., Euzenat, J.: Ontology matching: state of the art and future challenges. IEEE Transactions on Knowledge and Data Engineering 25(1), 158–176 (2013)
44. Giasson, F., D'Arcus, B.: The Bibliographic Ontology. Bibliographic Ontology Specification (2009), http://purl.org/ontology/bibo/
45. Brickley, D., Miller, L.: FOAF Vocabulary Specification 0.98. Marco Polo edn. (2010), http://xmlns.com/foaf/spec/
46. McGuinness, D., van Harmelen, F. (eds.): OWL Web Ontology Language Overview, W3C Recommendation (2004), http://www.w3.org/TR/owl-features/
47. Isaac, A., Summers, E.: SKOS Simple Knowledge Organization System Primer. W3C Working Group Note (2009), http://www.w3.org/TR/skos-primer
48. Miles, A., Brickley, D.: SKOS Core Guide. W3C Working Group Note (2005), http://www.w3.org/TR/swbp-skos-core-guide
49. Manola, F., Miller, E.: RDF Primer, W3C Recommendation (2004), http://www.w3.org/TR/rdf-primer/
50. Beckett, D. (ed.): RDF/XML Syntax Specification, W3C Recommendation (2004), http://www.w3.org/TR/rdf-syntax-grammar
51. Dargam, F., Zaraté, P., Ribeiro, R., Liu, S., Hernandez, J., Delibasic, B.: EURO Working Group on Decision Support Systems: Newsletter n°11, Research Report, IRIT/RR–2013-26–FR, IRIT (2013), https://websecu.irit.fr/rapports_newsletter_EWG-DSS
52. Delibasic, B., Jovanovic, M., Vukicevic, M., Suknovic, M., Obradovic, Z.: Component-based decision trees for classification. Intelligent Data Analysis 15(5), 671–693 (2011)
53. Antal, T., Krapivsky, P.L.: Weight-driven growing networks. Physical Review E 71, 026103 (2005)
54. Barrat, A., Barthelemy, M., Vespignani, A.: Weighted evolving networks: coupling topology and weight dynamics. Physical Review Letters 92, 228701 (2004)
55. Boccaletti, S., Latora, V., Moreno, Y., Chavez, M., Hwang, D.U.: Complex networks: structure and dynamics. Physics Reports 424, 175 (2006)
56. Brandes, U.: On variants of shortest-path betweenness centrality and their generic computation. Social Networks – An International Journal of Structural Analysis 30(2), 136–145 (2008)
57. Heidler, R.: Cognitive and social structure of the elite collaboration network of astrophysics: a case study on shifting network structures. Minerva 49, 461–488 (2011)

58. Jankovic, M., Zaraté, P.: Discrepancies and Analogies in Artificial Intelligence and Engineering Design Approaches in Addressing Collaborative Decision Making. International Journal of Decision Support System Technology 3(2), 1–14 (2011)

59. Liu, S., Duffy, A.H.B., Whitfield, R.I., Boyle, I.M.: Integration of decision support systems to improve decision support performance. Knowledge and Information Systems - An International Journal 22(3), 261–286 (2010)

60. Opsahl, T., Agneessens, F., Skvoretz, J.: Node centrality in weighted networks: generalizing degree and shortest paths. Social Networks – An International Journal of Structural Analysis 32(3), 245–251 (2010)

61. Shim, J.P., Warkentin, M., Courtney, J.F., Power, D.J., Sharda, R., Carlsson, C.: Past, present and future of decision support technology. Decision Support Systems 33(2), 111–126 (2002)

62. Weimao, K., Simas, T.: Mapping a Local Web Domain. In: Proceedings of the 11th International Conference on Information Visualisation, IV, July 2-6, pp. 228–231. IEEE Computer Society, Zürich (2007)

63. Yook, S.H., Jeong, H., Barabasi, A.L., Tu, Y.: Weighted evolving networks. Physical Review Letters 86, 5835 (2001)

64. Zheng, D., Trimper, S., Zheng, B., Hui, P.M.: Weighted scale-free networks with stochastic assignments. Physical Review E 67(4), 040102 (2003)

65. Hu, C., Racherla, P., Singh, N.: Developing a Knowledge-Based System Using Domain-Specific Ontologies and Experts: The eSAFE Case Study for the Event Management. In: ENTER 2006, pp. 273–284 (2006)

Testing the Seddon Model of Information System Success in an E-Learning Context: Implications for Evaluating DSS

Sean Eom

Accounting Department, Southeast Missouri State University, Cape Girardeau, USA

Abstract. Evaluation of DSS is concerned with analyzing costs and benefits of DSS before and after DSS development and implementation. The unique nature of DSS evaluation is that although some DSS provide substantial cost savings and profit increases, measurements of benefits of DSS have been problematic as quantification of the positive impacts of the improved decision process is difficult. In the early 1990s, DeLone and McLean presented the information systems (IS) success model as a framework and model for conceptualizing and operationalizing IS (including DSS) success. The DM model is one of the widely recognized IS models based on a systematic review of 180 studies which investigated over 100 success measures. An important assumption of the DM model is that it is the model to explain IS success in a voluntary IS use context. Due to the results of many empirical research results which do not support the positive relationship between system use and other constructs, Seddon presents a respecified and extended version of DeLone and McLean's model. We empirically tested the respecified version of the DM IS success model in an e-learning context, which is a strictly involuntary use setting. The paper provides an empirical evidence to support an alternative DSS evaluation model that can replace "system use" as the pivotal element of IS success model, with "perceived usefulness".

Keywords: the DeLone and McLean model, information systems success, DSS evaluation, Structural Equation model, the Seddon Model, WarpPLS.

Introduction

Evaluation of DSS is concerned with analyzing costs and benefits of DSS before and after DSS development and implementation. The unique nature of DSS evaluation is that although some DSS provide substantial cost savings and profit increases, measurements of benefits of DSS have been problematic as quantification of the positive impacts of the improved decision process is difficult. Therefore, DSS evaluation research deals with the measurements of the following benefits before and after DSS implementation: decision outputs, changes in the decision process, changes in managers' concepts of the decision situation, procedural changes, cost/benefit analysis, service measures and managers' assessment of the system's value [1].

Evaluating DSS involves examining multi-dimensional attributes associated with the value of DSS though the analysis of costs and benefits. The multidimensional attributes include decision output (actual results of the decisions such as profit, cost

J.E. Hernández et al. (Eds.): EWG-DSS 2012, LNBIP 164, pp. 19–33, 2013.

reduction, etc.), changes in the decision process, and the quality of decision support systems. Since the early 1970s, a large number of field and laboratory studies have been conducted to evaluate the effectiveness of DSS in terms of decision quality, decision confidence, costs and benefits, etc. All these studies have produced inconsistent and inconclusive results with regard to the positive impacts of DSS users over the users without DSS.

The other stream of information systems (IS) evaluation research examined the relationship between user involvement and IS success [2] and the relationship between user satisfaction and systems use [3]. These studies concluded that user involvement has positive relationships with system quality and system acceptance and that user satisfaction with the system will lead to greater system usage. However, many prior research papers failed to identify the positive relationship between system use and decision quality [4], and between systems use and decision time [5-7].

Aldag and Power[4] conducted a laboratory study on DSS effectiveness. They tested the effects of computerized decision aids on the quality of decision. In doing so, individual differences are incorporated as an independent variable to find correlations of attitude toward the decision aid to individual-difference indices. Based on the review of a number of prior research papers [8-15], Aldag and Power conducted a laboratory study, in which business students were instructed to analyze ill-structured strategic management cases with or without DSS. An interactive heuristic program was used to solve a case problem by two groups of students. The result of the Aldag and Power study detected no significant differences in performances, although user attitudes toward the computer-based decision aid were favorable and users gained more decision confidence. Their study suggested that user affect should not be used as a proxy for decision quality. DSS must be adopted with caution in that if such decision aids result in positive user affect and heightened decision confidence without corresponding improvements in decision quality, DSS may be dysfunctional.

Sharda and others [7] reviewed the results of 24 prior studies: four representative case studies [16-19], six field studies [1, 20-24], three field tests [25-27], and 11 laboratory studies [4-6, 28-35]. Field and laboratory test-based studies reached inconclusive results with regard to the positive impacts of DSS users over the users without DSS. Further, Sharda and others [7] conducted an experimental investigation using an executive decision making game. It was played by two sections of business strategy course students to find out that the groups with DSS made significantly more effective decisions, examined more alternatives, and exhibited a higher confidence level in their decisions than their non-DSS counterparts.

1   The DM Model of IS Success

In the early 1990s, DeLone and McLean presented the information systems (IS) success model as a framework and model for conceptualizing and operationalizing IS (including DSS) success [36]. DeLone and McLean presented a more integrated view of the concept of IS success and formulated a more comprehensive model of IS success (hereafter referred to as the DM model). The DM model is one of the widely recognized IS models based on a systematic review of 180 studies which investigated over 100 success measures. This model was based on six major categories of success measures, which are interrelated and interdependent. They are system quality, information quality, use, user satisfaction, individual impact, and organizational impact. Since the DM model was published without empirical testing, it has been successfully adopted and empirically tested to validate multidimensional relationships among the measures of IS success

Later the DM model was extended. The extended model clarified the meaning of IS use. It introduced four new variables (expectations, consequences, perceived usefulness, and net benefits to society) and reassembled the links among the variables.

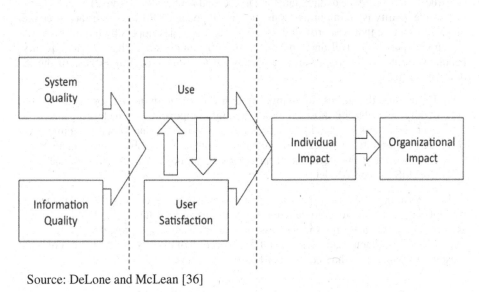

Source: DeLone and McLean [36]

Fig. 1. DeLone and McLean's Model of IS Success

An important assumption of the DM model is that it is the model to explain IS success in a voluntary IS use context. Due to the voluntariness of IS use, the "use" of the system is in the center of the model. The DM model has been empirically tested in a voluntary IS use context [37], a quasi-voluntary IS use context[38], and a mandatory information system context[39]. Moreover, numerous other studies tested the DM model in many different areas such as e-commerce systems [40], organizational memory information systems [41], enterprise resource planning (ERP) [42], health club industry [43], customer relationship management [44, 45], ERP Systems in China [46], online community [47], e-Government systems [48], and Spanish executive information systems(EIS) [49].

The study of Rai, et al. concluded that the DM model has explanatory power and therefore the model has merit for explaining IS success in a quasi-voluntary IS use context. The study of Livari concluded that perceived system quality and information quality are significant predictors of user satisfaction. But his study failed to support the positive association between system use and user satisfaction and between system use and individual impact in a mandatory environment.

As reviewed above, due to the voluntary nature of DSS, DSS effectiveness research has focused on the identification of relationships between DSS usage and performance, individual impact, and satisfaction. Due to the results of many empirical research results which do not support the positive relationship between system use and other constructs, Seddon presents a respecified and extended version of DeLone and McLean's model (figure 3). He maintained that the inclusion of both variance and process interpretations in the DM model leads to so many potentially confusing meanings. His respecified model of IS success clarified the meaning of *IS Use* and introduced four new variables (*Expectations, Consequences, Perceived Usefulness, and Net Benefits to Society*). Five years later, the original DM model expanded and updated to include several other constructs such as service quality, intention to use, and net benefits (figure 2).

Service quality is an important construct in the updated DM model. It measures the quality of service that was provided to support end user developers by the information systems department. DeLone and McLean [50] emphasized that service quality becomes the most important variable only when measuring overall success of the IS department (p.18).

> To measure the success of a single system, "information quality" or "system quality" may be the most important quality component. For measuring the overall success of the IS department, as opposed to individual systems, "service quality" may become the most important variable. Once again, context should dictate the appropriate specification and application of the D&M IS Success Model.

In e-learning context, the instructors is the end user developers. IS department's prompt service from its knowledgeable IS employee is important, but e-learning systems' success measures the success of e-learning systems indicated by learning outcomes and student satisfaction, not the success of the IS department. For that reason, this paper uses the Seddon model instead of the extended DM model.

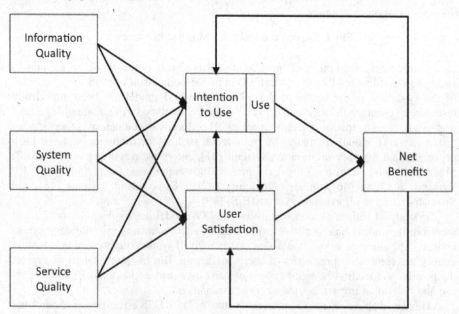

Fig. 2. DeLone and McLean's Expanded and Updated Model of IS Success [50]

The purpose of this paper is to empirically test the validity of the Seddon model in an e-learning environment in order to examine the applicability of the Seddon model in a mandatory IS use context. As discussed earlier, the DM model failed to support the positive association between system use and user satisfaction and between system use and individual impact in a mandatory environment. Decision support systems today are being used in a voluntary, quasi-voluntary, and mandatory context. Empirical testing of the Seddon model in a mandatory environment may help us assess its suitability as an evaluation tool for DSS success.

The rest of this chapter is organized into several sections. The following section briefly describes the Seddon model of IS success and prior literature on course delivery technologies and e-learning success. Course delivery technologies are part of a comprehensive array of dependent variables that affect the success of e-learning systems. The next section presents the research model to be tested. The survey instrument is discussed in the next section. It is followed by a discussion of structural equation modeling (SEM) methodology and results of the analysis. It is followed by conclusion, implications for evaluating DSS success, and limitations and future research.

2   The Seddon Model of IS Success

The research model we tested is the respecified version of DeLone and McLean's Model of IS Success.

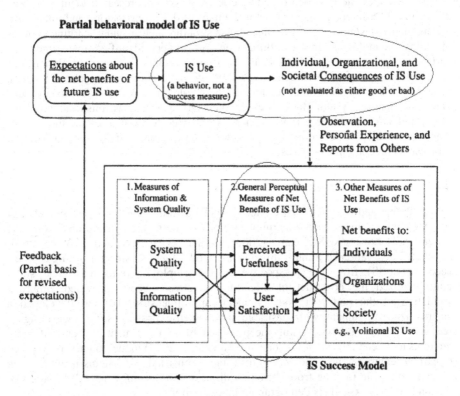

Fig. 3. Respecified version of DeLone and McLean's model [51]

Five years later, Seddon presents a respecified and extended version of DeLone and McLean's model. Seddon concludes [51] that:

> Now, having worked with the model for some years, and having tested part of it empirically, it has become apparent that the inclusion of both variance and process interpretations in their model leads to so many potentially confusing meanings that the value of the model is diminished. By clarifying the meaning of *IS Use,* introducing four new variables (*Expectations, Consequences, Perceived Usefulness, and Net Benefits to Society*), and reassembling the links between the variables, it has been possible to develop the re-specified d and slightly extended model of IS Use & IS Success.

3   Learning Management Systems and E-Learning Success

During the past decades, we have seen an increase in empirical research studies to identify the success factors of e-learning systems. The majority of e-learning research has focused on the two research streams (a) outcome comparison studies with classroom-based learning; and (b) studies examining potential predictors of e-learning success or e-learning outcomes [52]. The quality of e-learning empirical research has also improved substantially during the past two decades. Many frameworks for e-learning education in business have been developed or adopted from other disciplines.

The review of the past two decades' e-learning systems research identified three dimensions of e-learning systems factor: human (students, instructors, and interaction among them), design (course contents, course structures, etc.), and e-learning systems including technologies. In each dimension, researchers identified many indicator variables. For example, students can be further sub-classified into sub-dimensions such as learning styles, intelligence, self-efficacy, motivation, self-regulated learning behaviors, etc. The technological dimension of e-learning success factors includes many information systems tools such as Web 2.0 technologies, push technologies, blogs, and wikis, to name a few. Readers are referred to [52] to review the various empirical studies to examine the impact of these tools and human and design dimensions on e-learning success.

4   Survey Instrument

Wang, Wang, and She [53] first explored whether traditional IS success models can be extended to investigate e-learning systems success in organizational contexts. Based on DeLone and McLean's (2003) updated IS success model, Wang, et al. developed and validated a multi-dimensional model for assessing e-learning systems success (ELSS) from the perspective of the employee (e-learner). The study conceptualized the construct of e-learning systems success, provided empirical validation of the construct and its underlying dimensionality, and developed a standardized instrument with desirable psychometric properties for measuring e-learning systems success. Using the proposed ELSS instrument, the current study attempts to extend the use of DeLone and McLean's (2003) model to university-based e-learning environments. The survey instrument consisted of 35 items using a seven point Likert scale ranging from "strongly disagree" to "strongly agree." In addition, respondents were asked six demographic-type questions.

The population was undergraduate and graduate students that were enrolled in an online course at a large university located in the Midwest United States. Invitations to reply to the survey were administered online at the time of log-in to 2,156 unique students. Of those students invited, 809 students volunteered responses with 674 surveys being complete and usable for a response rate of 31.3%.

5   Research Model

The research model we tested is the Respecified version of DeLone and McLean's model [51]. The research model (Figure 4) examines the relationships among five constructs. The three independent constructs are system quality, information quality, and benefits. The mediating construct is perceived usefulness. The dependent construct is user satisfaction.

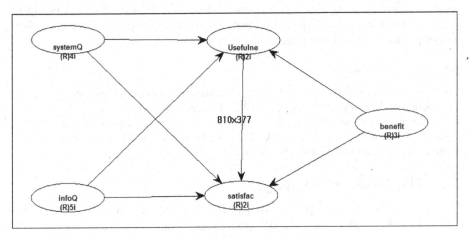

Fig. 4. Research Model

6   Research Methodology

The seven sets of hypotheses were tested using WarpPLS. WarpPLS is a variance-based (a.k.a. partial least square-based) structural equation modeling software. PLS-based SEM yields robust results despite that it does not have measurement, distributional, or sample size assumptions [54, 55]. Despite the fact that there exist non-linear relationships between latent variables in social and natural sciences, most of SEM software do not take the non-linear relationships among latent variables into account when producing path coefficients and other statistical outputs. Unlike other PLS-based SEM software such as PLS-graph and smart PLS, WarpPLS identifies non-linear relationships among latent variables [56].

6.1   System Quality and Information Quality

The IS success model [36, 50] and the e-learning success model [57] posit that the success of IS and e-learning systems is dependent on the intervening variables (user satisfaction and system use), which are in turn dependent on the quality of information, system, and service.

System quality is the quality of the information system itself. The quality of the information system is measured by multiple distinctive characteristics of the information system itself. Specifically, the information system is a set of software, hardware (input, processing, output, and telecommunication devices), procedure, data, and people interacting together. Prior empirical studies used a wide range of empirical measures of user interface attributes such as convenience of access, ease of use, ease of learning, and usefulness of functionality. Empirical measures related to output include reliability with less error rate and response time.

6.2   Perceived Usefulness

System use has been considered as a factor that influences the system success in the past decades and has been used by a number of researchers. [36, 38, 50, 57]. However, many studies failed to detect the relationships between system use and user satisfaction and benefits. Consequently, the Seddon model replaced system use with perceived usefulness. We hypothesize that perceived usefulness is a construct that will be positively related to e-learner satisfaction.

6.3   User Satisfaction

There is abundant prior research that examines the relationships between user satisfaction and individual impact [38, 39, 58].   A study of Eom et al. [59] examined the determinants of students' satisfaction and their perceived learning outcomes in the context of university online courses. Their study found that user satisfaction is a significant predictor of learning outcomes.

7   The Results of the Analysis

WarpPLS produces average path coefficient (APC) of .222 with p < .001, average R-Squared (ARS) of .586 with p <.0001, and average variance inflation factor (AVI) of 3.710. Since we aim to test 7 hypotheses, they are not so critical. However, these values indicate the model has an excellent fit.

7.1   Measurement (Outer) Model Results

Due to the fact that the latent variable can be only indirectly measureable by using more than one observable variable, the issue of *validity* in SEM is an important matter. Validity is concerned with the extent to which each observed variable accurately define the construct. Each measurement item on a survey instrument is assumed to reflect only one latent variable and each item is related to one construct better than to any others [60].

There are two elements of construct (factorial) validity: convergent validity and discriminant validity. Convergent validity is defined as the extent to which indicators of a latent variable converge or share high proportions of variance in common. Our measurement model has acceptable convergent validity since each of all 17 indicator variables has p-values less than .001 and the factor loadings ranges from .799 to .961. For reflective indicators, p-values less than .05 are desirable. The minimum threshold values of the factor loadings are equal to or greater than .5.[61]   Table 1 shows factor loadings. All indicator (observed) variables, q1 through q20, load highly on their assigned factors, .5 or higher. Ideally, they should be .7 or higher. Additionally, each of the measurement items, q1 through q20, loads with an acceptable p-value of .001 or less. WarpPLS generates factor validity information of AVE (Average Variance Extracted).

To establish discriminant validity, we compared the square root of average variance extracted (AVE) for each construct with the correlations among constructs (Table 2). If the square root of each AVE is much larger than any correlation among any pair of latent variables, and is greater than .50 [60, 62, 63], then the validity of the measurement model is established. Overall, the measurement model results provided strong support for the factorial, convergent, and discriminant validities and reliability of the measures used in the study.

Table 1. Convergent and Discriminant Validity and Reliability of the Measurement Model

Constructs & Associated Variables	Measurement Items	Factor Loadings
System Quality ave=.850		
Q1	The system is always available	0.799
Q2	The system is user-friendly	0.896
Q4	The system has an attractive feature that appeal to the user	0.856
Q5	The system provides high-speed information access	0.846
Information Quality ave=.908		
Q6	The system provides info. that is exactly what you need	0.915
Q7	The system provides info. that is relevant to learning	0.908
Q8	The system provides sufficient information	0.934
Q9	The system provides information that is easy to understand	0.917
Q10	The system provides up-to-date information	0.865
Perceived Usefulness Ave=.875		
Q12	I depend upon the system	0.875
Q20	The system is an important and valuable aid to me in the performance of my class work	0.875
User Satisfaction Ave=.961		
Q15	I think the system is very helpful	0.961
Q16	Overall, I am satisfied with the system	0.961
System Benefits Ave=.955		
Q17	The system has a positive impact on my learning	0.938
Q18	Overall, the performance of the system is good	0.967
Q19	Overall, the system is successful	0.961

Table 2. Correlations among latent variable Scores (Square Roots of AVE shown on Diagonal)

	System Quality	Info Quality	System Use	Satisfaction	Benefits
System Quality	**0.850**				
Info Quality	0.831	**0.908**			
Perceived Usefulness	0.614	0.667	**0.875**		
Satisfaction	0.796	0.825	0.709	**0.961**	
Benefits	0.803	0.834	0.737	0.916	**0.955**

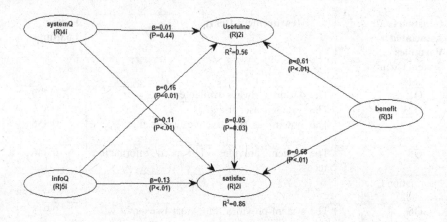

Fig. 5. Structural (Inner) Model Results

Table 3. Structural (Inner) Model Results

	Path Coefficients	P-value	Sig. Level
Effects on Perceived Usefulness ($R^2 = .56$)			
System quality	+.01	+0.44	ns
Info. Quality	+.16	+0.01	***
Net Benefits	+.61	<+.01	***
Effects on User Satisfaction ($R^2 = .834$)			
System Quality	+.11	<+.01	***
Info. Quality	+.13	<. +01	***
Perceived Usefulness	+.05	+0.03	**
Net Benefits	+.68	<+.01	***

**** $p < .001$, *** $p < .010$, ** $p < .050$, * $p < .100$ ns not significant

As figure 5 shows, one hypothesized relationship involving perceived usefulness construct is not supported (between system quality and perceived usefulness). Other six hypothesized relationships are supported at the significance level of $p<0.10$, except one with $p<.05$. The results show that the structural model explains 56 percent of the variance in the perceived usefulness construct and 86 percent of the variance in the user satisfaction construct.

8   Implications for Evaluating DSS Success

We examined the respecified version of the Seddon IS success model in an e-learning context, which is a strictly involuntary use setting. In the Seddon model, the "use" is no longer be a critical construct in evaluating DSS success in that a substantial portion of DSS published seem to be mandatory or semi-mandatory. Moreover, Seddon [51] believes that "system use" should be deleted as a success variable in the causal success model. He further argues that "system use" does not cause impacts and benefits. To respond to Seddon, DeLone and McLean strongly defended the "system use" as an important indication of IS success. The DM model in the 1990s is evolved after the demise of two research streams of information systems (IS) evaluation research [3, 64]. The paper provides an empirical evidence to support an alternative DSS evaluation model that can replace "system use" as the pivotal element of IS success model, with "perceived usefulness". System use in e-learning was empirically tested and it failed to detect a positive relationship with e-learner satisfaction [65].

9   Limitations and Further Research

The current study could have been better if there were more indicator variables in the perceived usefulness and user satisfaction constructs. Currently, these constructs have two indicator variables. Besides, net benefits could be measured more specifically to individuals and organizations, respectively. A possible future research direction is to test the expanded and updated model of IS success (Figure 2) and compare its results with the results of the full version of the Seddon model (Figure 3). These two competing models of IS success deserve further future testing to clarify the relationships among various constructs.

References

[1] Keen, P.G.W., Scott Morton, M.S.: Decision Support Systems: An Organizational Perspective. Addison-Wesley, Reading (1978)

[2] Ives, B., Olson, M.H.: User Involvement in Information Systems: A Critical Review of the Empirical Literature (1980), unpublished paper

[3] Baroudi, J.J., Olsen, M.H., Ives, B.: An empirical study of the impact of user involvement on systems usage and information satisfaction. Communications of the ACM 29(3), 232–238 (1986)

[4] Aldag, R.J., Power, D.J.: An Empirical Assessment of Computer-Assisted Decision Analysis. Decision Sciences 17(4), 572–588 (1986)

[5] Benbasat, I., Schroeder, R.G.: An Experimental Investigation of Some MIS Design Variables. MIS Quarterly 1(1), 37–50 (1977)

[6] Benbasat, I., Dexter, A.S.: Individual Differences in the Use of Decision Support Aids. Journal of Accounting Research 20(1), 1–11 (1982)

[7] Sharda, R., Bar, S.H., McDonnell, J.C.: Decision Support System Effectiveness: A Review and Empirical Test. Management Science 34(2), 139–159 (1988)

[8] Bronner, F., de Hoog, R.: Non-Expert Use of a Computerized Decision Aid. In: Humphreys, P., Svenson, O., Vari, A. (eds.) Analyzing and Aiding Decision Processes, pp. 281–299. Adadimiai Kiadó, Budapest (1983)

[9] Cats-Baril, W.L.: Cognitive Aid and Decision Support Systems: An Empirical Investigation of three-Dimensions. Ph.D. Dissertation, Operations and Information Management, University of Wisconsin-Madison (University Microfilms International No.8225636), Madison, WI (1982)

[10] Christen, F.G., Samet, M.G.: Empirical Evaluation of a Decision-analytic Aid, Final Technical Report PFTR-1066-80-1, Perceptronics, Inc., Woodland Hills, CA (1980)

[11] Humphreys, P., McFadden, W.: Experiences with MAUD: Aiding Decision Structuring versus Bootstrapping The Decision Maker. Acta Psychologica 45(1-3), 51–69 (1980)

[12] John, R.S., von Winterfeldt, D., Edwards, W.: The Quality and user acceptance of Multiattribute utility analysis performed by Computer and Analyst. In: Humphreys, P., Svenson, O., Vari, A. (eds.) Analyzing and Aiding Decision Processes. Adkademiai Kiadó, Budapest (1983)

[13] Paine, F.T., Naumes, W.: Organizational strategy and policy. W. B. Saunders, Philadelphia (1978)

[14] Pearl, J., Leal, A., Saleh, J.: GODDESS: A Goal-Directed Decision Structuring System. IEEE Transactions on Pattern Analysis & Machine Intelligence PAMI-4(3), 250–262 (1982)

[15] Power, D.J., Rose, G.: Improving Decision Making behavior Using The Hewlett-Packard, access System, pp. 47–49 (2000)

[16] Ferguson, R.L., Jones, C.H.: A Computer Aided Decision System. Management Science 15(10), B550–B561 (1969)

[17] Simon, H.A.: The New Science of Management Decisions, Revised edn. Prentice Hall, Englewood Cliffs (1977)

[18] Bass, B.: Organizational Decision Making. Richard D. Irwin, Homewood (1983)

[19] Horwitt, E.: DSS: Effective Relief for Frustrated Management. Business Computer Systems 7, 44–58 (1984)

[20] Garrity, J.T.: Top Management and Computer Profits. Harvard Business Review 41(4), 172–174 (1963)

[21] Dean, N.J.: The Computer Comes of Age. Harvard Business Review 46(1), 83–91 (1968)

[22] Gallagher, C.A.: Perceptions of the Value of a Management Information System. Academy of Management Journal 17(1), 46–55 (1974)

[23] Alter, S.L.: Decision Support Systems: Current Practice and Continuing Challenges. Addison-Wesley, Reading (1980)

[24] Wagner, G.R.: Realizing DSS Benefits with The IFPS Planning Language

[25] Fudge, W.K., Lodish, L.M.: Evaluation of the Effectiveness of a Model Based Salesman's Planning System by Field Experimentation. Interfaces 8(1/2), 97–106 (1977)

[26] Edelman, F.: Managers, Computer Systems, and Productivity. MIS Quarterly 5(3), 1–18 (1981)

[27] Gochenouer, J.E.: An Empirical Study of the Impact of a Decision Support Language on Knowledge Workers. Ph.D. Dissertation, Florida Institute of Technology, Melbourne, FL (1985)

[28] Joyner, R., Tunstall, K.: Computer Augmented Organizational Problem Solving. Management Science 17(4), B212–B225 (1970)

[29] King, W.R., Rodriguez, J.I.: Evaluating Management Information Systems. MIS Quarterly 2(3), 43–51 (1978)

[30] Chakravarti, D., Mitchell, A.A., Staelin, R.: Judgment Based Marketing Decision Models: An Experimental Investigation of the Decision Calculus Approach. Management Science 25(3), 251–263 (1979)

[31] McIntyre, S.H.: An Experimental Study of the Impact of Judgment-Based Marketing Models. Management Science 28(1), 17–33 (1982)

[32] Dickmeyer, N.: Measuring the Effects of a University Planning Decision Aid. Management Science 29(6), 673–685 (1983)

[33] Eckel, N.L.: The Impact of Probabilistic Information on Decision Behaviour and Performance in an Experimental Game. Decision Sciences 14(4), 483–502 (1983)

[34] Goslar, M.D., Green, G.I., Hughes, T.H.: Decision Support Systems: An Empirical Assessment for Decision Making. Decision Sciences 17(1), 79–91 (1986)

[35] Cats-Baril, W.L., Huber, G.P.: Decision Support Systems for Ill-Structured Problems: An Empirical Study. Decision Sciences 18(3), 350–372 (1987)

[36] DeLone, W.H., McLean, E.R.: Information System Success: The Quest for The Dependent Variable. Information Systems Research 3(1), 60–95 (1992)

[37] Carlsson, S.A., Skog, L.-M., Tona, O.: An IS Success Evaluation of a DSS in a Police Organization. In: Respício, A., Adam, F., Phillips-Wren, G., Teixeira, C., Telhada, J. (eds.) Bridging the Socio-technical Gap in Decision Support Systems. Frontiers in Artificial Intelligence and Applications, pp. 443–454. IOS Press, Amsterdam (2010)

[38] Rai, A., Lang, S.S., Welker, R.B.: Assessing the Validity of IS Success Models: An Empirical Test and Theoretical Analysis. Information Systems Research 13(1), 50–69 (2002)

[39] Livari, J.: An Empirical Test of the DeLone-McLean Model of Information System Success. The DATA BASE for Advances in Information Systems 36(2), 8–27 (2005)

[40] Molla, A., Licker, P.S.: E-Commerce Systems Success: An Attempt to Extend and Respecify the DeLone and McLean Model of IS Success. Journal of Electronic Commerce Research 2(4), 131–141 (2001)

[41] Jennex, M., Olfman, L., Panthawi, P., Park, Y.-T.: An Organizational Memory Information Systems Success Model: An Extension of DeLone and McLean's I/S Success Model. In: Proceedings of the Thirty-First Annual Hawaii International Conference on System Sciences, pp. 157–165. IEEE Computer Society, Washington, D.C (1998)

[42] Bernroider, E.W.N.: IT governance for enterprise resource planning supported by the DeLone–McLean model of information systems success. Information & Management 45(5), 257–269 (2008)

[43] Skok, W., Kophamel, A., Richardson, I.: Diagnosing information systems success: importance–performance maps in the health club industry. Information & Management 38(7), 409–419 (2001)

[44] Avlonitis, G.J., Panagopoulos, N.G.: Antecedents and Consequences of CRM Technology Acceptance in the Sales Force. Industrial Marketing Management 34(4), 355–368 (2005)

[45] Wilson, H., Daniel, E., McDonald, M.: Factors for Success in Customer Relationship Management (CRM) Systems. Journal of Marketing Management 18(1/2), 193–219 (2002)

[46] Zhang, Z., Lee, M.K.O., Huang, P., Zhang, L., Huang, X.: A framework of ERP systems implementation success in China: An empirical study. International Journal of Production Economics 98(1), 58–80 (2005)

[47] Lin, H.-F., Lee, G.-G.: Determinants of success for online communities: an empirical study. Behaviour & Information Technology 25(6), 479–488 (2006)

[48] Wang, Y.-S., Liao, Y.-W.: Assessing eGovernment systems success: A validation of the DeLone and McLean model of information systems success. Government Information Quarterly 25(4), 717–733 (2008)

[49] Roldán, J.L., Leal, A.: A Validation Test of an Adaptation of the DeLone and McLean's Model in the Spanish EIS Field. In: Cano, J.J. (ed.) Critical Reflections on Information Systems: A Systemic Approach, pp. 66–84. IDEA Group Publishing, Hershey (2003)

[50] DeLone, W.H., McLean, E.R.: The DeLone and McLean model of information systems success: A ten-year update. Journal of Management Information Systems 19(4), 9–30 (2003)

[51] Seddon, P.B.: A respecification and Extension of The DeLone and McLean Model of Is Success. Information Systems Research 8(3), 240–253 (1997)

[52] Arbaugh, J.B., Godfrey, M.R., Johnson, M., Pollack, B.L., Niendorf, B., Wresch, W.: Research in online and blended learning in the business disciplines: Key findings and possible future directions. Internet and Higher Education 12, 71–87 (2009)

[53] Wang, Y.-S., Wang, H.-Y., Shee, D.Y.: Measuring e-learning systems success in an organizational context: Scale development and validation. Computers in Human Behavior 23(4), 1792–1808 (2007)

[54] Ashill, N.J.: An Introduction to Structural Equation Modeling (SEM) and the Partial Least Squares (PLS) Methodology. In: Eom, S.B., Arbaugh, J.B. (eds.) Student Satisfaction and Learning Outcomes in E-Learning: An Introduction to Empirical Research. IGI Global, Hershey (2011)

[55] Lohmoller, J.: Latent Variable Path Modeling with Partial Least Squares. Physica-Verlag, Heidelberg (1989)

[56] Kock, N.: Using WarpPLS in e-Collaboration Studies: Descriptive Statistics, Settings, and Key Analysis Results. International Journal of e-Collaboration 7(2), 1–18 (2011)

[57] Holsapple, C.W., Lee-Post, A.: Defining, assessing, and promoting e-learning success: An information systems perspective. Decision Sciences Journal of Innovative Education 4(1), 67–85 (2006)

[58] Doll, W.J., Torkzadeh, G.: The Measurement of End User Computing Satisfaction. MIS Quarterly 12(2), 259–274 (1988)

[59] Eom, S.B., Ashill, N., Wen, H.J.: The Determinants of Students' Perceived Learning Outcome and Satisfaction in University Online Education: An Empirical Investigation. Decision Sciences Journal of Innovative Education 4(2), 215–236 (2006)

[60] Gefen, D., Straub, D.: A Practical guide to factorial validity using PLS-Graph: Tutorial and annotated example. Communications of the Association for Information Systems 16, 91–109 (2005)

[61] Kock, N.: WarPLS 3.0 User Manual, ScriptWarp Systems, Laredo, TX (2012)

[62] Chin, W.W.: The partial least squares approach to structural equation modeling. In: Marcoulides, G.A. (ed.) Modern Methods for Business Research, pp. 295–336. Lawrence Erlbaum Associates, Mahwah (1998)

[63] Fornell, C.R., Larcker, D.: Evaluating Structural Equation Models with Unobservable Variables and Measurement Error. Journal of Marketing Research 18(1), 39–50 (1981)

[64] Ives, B., Olson, M.H.: User Involvement and MIS Success: A Review of Research. Management Science 30(5), 580–603 (1984)

[65] Eom, S.B.: Testing the Delone-Mclean Model of Information System Success in an E-Learning Context: Implications for Evaluating Mandatory DSS. In: Respício, A., Burstein, F. (eds.) Fusing Decision Support Systems into the Fabric of the Context, pp. 15–26. IOS Press, Amsterdam (2012)

The Benefits of SaaS-Based Enterprise Systems for SMEs - A Literature Review

Gwendolin Schäfer, Marion Schulze, Yahaya Yusuf, and Ahmed Musa

University of Central Lancashire, Preston PR1 2HE, UK
{GSchaefer,MSchulze,YYusuf,AMusa}@uclan.ac.uk
http://www.uclan.ac.uk

Abstract. A new affordable generation of Software-as-a-Service based Enterprise Systems is now available for small and medium sized enterprises and makes this topic highly significant. It has been identified that those enterprises can only gain a limited amount of benefits from Enterprise Systems in contrast to large enterprises, which can take advantage of a greater benefits range. The extent to which these benefits can be realised is still unclear. The aim of this paper is therefore to identify, classify, interpret and discuss the current academic knowledge of Enterprise Systems benefits for small and medium sized enterprises. This paper clarifies the nature of such systems and presents a systematic literature review, investigating research on the benefits of Enterprise Systems and important components of it, namely Enterprise Resource Planning, Supply Chain Management, Supplier Relationship Management, and Customer Relationship Management. The result of this research offers a first framework for potential benefits of Software-as-a-Service based Enterprise Systems.

Keywords: Software-as-a-Service (SaaS), enterprise systems for SMEs, benefits, literature review, ERP, supply chain.

1 Introduction

Enterprise Systems (ES) are "commercial software packages that enable the integration of transaction-oriented data and business processes throughout an organization (and perhaps eventually throughout the entire inter-organisational supply chain)" [1]. Another widely used term for an ES is 'ERP II' [2], indicating the importance of Enterprise Resource Planning (ERP) as core component of ES. This paper will focus on four important ES components, namely ERP, Supply Chain Management (SCM), Supplier Relationship Management (SRM), and Customer Relationship Management (CRM).

The investigation of this topic is important because nowadays small and medium sized enterprises (SMEs) are exposed to increasing pressure to implement ES. This stems from customers who wish to connect the information flow of some or all participants of a supply chain. So far ES have been successful in large enterprises (LEs), but struggled to reach SMEs. A new technology, called Software-as-a-Service (SaaS), now allows for cheaper all-in-one ES solutions.

J.E. Hernández et al. (Eds.): EWG-DSS 2012, LNBIP 164, pp. 34–45, 2013.

The ERP market leaders for large organisations, namely Oracle, SAP and Microsoft [3], now target the SME market with this innovation. Therefore an urgent need of informing SMEs about the nature and benefits of SaaS-based arises.

No literature about benefits of SaaS-based ES and only very little literature about benefits of ES in general exists. However, a great variety of research was carried out about benefits of ERP and also some about other ES components. Nobody has yet summarised ES benefits for SMEs and distinguished between benefits dependent on the selected ES components. This paper intends to close some of this gap and to develop a framework for expected benefits of SaaS-based integrated enterprise systems (IES) for SMEs. This is done in order to inform SMEs about potential benefits of such systems and serves researchers as basis for further SaaS-based IES research. The aim of this paper is therefore to identify, classify, interpret and discuss the current academic knowledge of Enterprise Systems benefits for small and medium sized enterprises. The following research objectives are part of this study:

1. Clarify the nature of (SaaS-based) IES from the SME perspective
2. Summarise the body of knowledge about potential benefits of ES for SMEs
3. Identify research perspectives for future SaaS-based IES research

To achieve these objectives this paper is divided into three main sections. First, the nature of ES and its components will be explored. Second, the results of the literature review on benefits of ES will be presented. The third section will investigate how the result of the literature review might impact on SaaS-based IES research. In the conclusion it will be evaluated if the research objectives have been achieved, how these results serve practitioners and academics, and what still has to be researched.

2   The Nature of Enterprise Systems

To obtain a better understanding of the nature of ES, it is helpful to explore the historical development of Information Communication Technology (ICT) systems for business. After gaining this understanding, ES components will be explored in depth. Finally this section concludes with an overview of IES solutions for SMEs in the light of SaaS-based products.

2.1   History of Enterprise Systems

Historically, it can be distinguished between material requirement planning (MRP1), manufacturing resource planning (MRP2), ERP, and ES [4,5]. These systems support one company and ES provides support even beyond the own company. The invention of client-server systems allowed decentralised use of Personal Computers within a company, providing a massively improved user interface and performance compared to MRP1 and MRP2 systems. These new systems were called ERP. ERP can be defined as a "method for the effective planning and controlling of all the resources needed to take, make, ship and account for customer orders in a manufacturing, distribution or service company" [6]. Firstly, they integrate all business processes, not only planning and controlling but also execution. Secondly, users are able to share common practices throughout the enterprise [7]. Thirdly, users can share common data from one database and access real-time information [7]. This database is the condition for building an ERP system. Subsequently SaaS was invented [8], allowing a connection of systems via Internet and offering access to company software. This allowed the development of integrated software that can connect stakeholders and automate business processes across the supply chain. This new systems landscape is called ES or ERP 2 and will be explored in depth in the next sub-section.

2.2   Definition of Enterprise Systems (ES)

The main difference between ERP and ES is the scope of supported business processes. ERP only integrates intra-company processes whereas ES additionally supports business processes across companies. Therefore researchers (e.g. [2,5,9,10]) see ERP as a core component of ES. It was noted that there is a lack of agreed components of ES. This means that the academic literature mentions a whole range of possible components [2,5,9,10]. From this it can be established that ten different components could be implemented to advance an ERP system to become an ES. The limited scope of this research project makes it necessary to restrain the number of components that will be investigated. Therefore the focus is on solutions that are mentioned most often and are therefore considered as most important, namely ERP, SCM, SRM and CRM [2,5,9,10]. It is assumed that the remaining ES components have a minor significance for SMEs. In the following section SCM, SRM, and CRM will be defined for this research.

2.3   Definition of ES Components - SCM, CRM, and SRM ICT

It is can be distinguished between SCM as theoretical framework and SCM ICT as one condition to put this framework into practice [12,11]. SCM as theoretical framework can be defined as "the integration of key business processes from end-user to original suppliers that provides products, services, and information and hence add value for customers and other stakeholders" ([13], cited in: [14]) and "a set of practices aimed at managing and co-ordinating the supply chain" [15]. SCM ICT supports not only planning but also execution and monitoring processes like purchasing and demand fulfilment, but only on an operational level [12]. Many authors (e.g. [2,5,9,10,16]) define also CRM and SRM as two major components for SCM. The reason for this distinction could be that not all companies need SCM planning or material tracking but might want to connect their ICT with customers and vendors to improve their inter-organisational business processes. Therefore ES vendors offer these components separately.

"Customer Relationship Management [is a theoretical concept which] is the building of a profitable relationship between a business and its customers through effective one-on-one communication and customer service delivery leading to customer value" [17]. CRM provides functionalities for internet supported customer relations processes, sales and marketing processes and product and services enhancement, but also information for related business processes like production and operations, supplier relations, and process planning and support [18].

SRM is the IT-based composition of the operational and strategic procurement approach and the management of suppliers based on the overall procurement strategy [19]. Furthermore, it can be established that SRM is the counterpart of CRM, which operates upstream the supply chain [20].

After having clarified the components of ES that will be investigated in this study it has to be emphasised that from an SMEs point of view the term Enterprise System can describe a whole range of different system constellations. All constellations have in common that data are integrated and that there is at least one connection via Internet. This means that an ES has ERP as core component and the option of at least one additional ES component. The two or more components can be from the same vendor, called an all-in-one solution, or from different vendors, called a best-of-breed solution [21].

The following sub-section will give more insight into newest developments of the ES market for SMEs in the light of SaaS.

2.4 SaaS-Based ES for SMEs

Large ES vendors often argue that all-in-one solutions are better than best-of-breed solutions because they create a plug-and play systems when all partners in the supply chain use the same vendor. The ERP system market for large enterprises is dominated by Oracle, SAP, and Microsoft [3] and their ES solutions (e.g. SAP Business Suite) are complex and require considerable implementation (thirteen to eighteen months [3]) and maintenance effort. Therefore, many SMEs decided not to implement them, not even their less complex sister products for SMEs (e.g. SAP Business One). Aftercare and maintenance requires experienced specialists, who can be very costly. As a result, many SMEs carried on using legacy systems or less complex ERP systems from other vendors.

SaaS seems to have solved this problem from the ERP market leaders point of view. Vendors now offer SaaS-based ES for SMEs. These solutions are comprised of an ERP core with additional ES components, which vary from vendor to vendor. The main difference between all-in-one systems and other ES is that the new solution is one software including every component but only the required ones are selected to be implemented. Opposed to this, other ES require individual components software, which have to be implemented separately. In this study all-in-one solutions will be called Integrated Enterprise Systems. SAP offers SAP Business ByDesign (ByD), the most complex and only integrated solution at the moment.

This development poses a new decision problem for SMEs. Should they replace their current legacy systems or less complex ERP solutions by the currently only available SaaS-based IES from SAP? This all depends on the benefits such a system can provide. However, there is no overview of benefits of ES for SMEs.

This paper intends to close some of this gap. A systematic literature review investigates what is known about ES component benefits for SMEs. The following section will describe the results of the review.

3   The Benefits of Enterprise Systems for SMEs

3.1   Methodology of Literature Review

This article intends to identify benefits SMEs can achieve with SaaS-based ES. A systematic literature review was carried out and the current body of ES knowledge evaluated. For this purpose the SciVerse Scopus database was researched. It has to be noted that no research has been conducted for IES in SMEs yet.

Most literature was found on ERP benefits. The focus was therefore firstly on existing literature reviews of ERP in SMEs and new articles concerning benefits of ERP for SMEs [22]. Only seven articles focus on benefits realised by SMEs after implementing ERP [23,24,25,26,27,28,29]. Three of those articles are industry specific - two focus on the manufacturing industry and one on the public sector [26,28,29]. The latter article is also system specific, focusing on SAP software. The limited result for SMEs led to the decision to review general benefits of ERP as well. It was reviewed to compare findings with SME research. For SCM, CRM, and SRM only a limited amount of research on benefits could be found, mainly not even SME specific. The same can be stated for ES in general.

Results will be described in the following sub-sections. The final sub-section will evaluate their relevance for SaaS-based IES benefits in SMEs and summarise the relevant findings as framework for potential IES benefits for SMEs.

3.2   Results of Literature Review: ES Benefits

Koh et al. [30] used existing literature from top ranked journals, recognised research houses and vendors publishing about ERP and ES to collect secondary information. Besides that, primary research was carried out with the help of questionnaires that were sent to industry experts (implementers, functional [parent] users and suppliers). This was done to identify and rate the benefits adjusted from Shang and Seddons [31] benefits framework on a 5-point Likert scale. Mathrani and Viehland [23] also considered the viewpoints of industry experts, namely ES vendors, ES consultants and IT research firms to study the benefits of ES for SMEs. However, in comparison to the Koh et al.'s [30] article, interviews were carried out with the 10 participants. The outcome of the studies showed that the majority of ERP benefits can be transferred to enterprise systems. Though, not all benefits identified in the literature could be detected in the SME research. It was discovered that the amount of benefits of enterprise systems varies only to some extent from ERP benefits. Furthermore, an increase in intensity of benefits achieved could be declared for some. Another outcome was to identify the variance in perception between the three expert groups. Mathrani and Viehland [23] recommend further research into the different perspectives of SMEs and consultants towards benefits of ES for SMEs.

3.3   Results of Literature Review: ES Components' Benefits for SMEs

Federici [25] studied five benefits of ERP systems for SMEs. It was evaluated to what extent the benefits could be reached and if they were related to any factors. The result showed that SMEs of every sector and size are able to benefit from ERP. It was also displayed that SMEs may obtain the same benefits as LEs. Kale et al. [24] used questionnaires and interviews aimed at prioritising benefits after ERP implementation for data collection. The authors provided a list of benefits and CSF with the possibility for expansion. Frequency analysis was used to evaluate the collected data and show the importance of benefits.

Wang and Sedera [32] developed a framework of SCM benefits based on an extensive literature review and website analysis in 2011 and conducted one case study in a LE to test which benefits could be realised. This framework has not been tested yet for SMEs. Previous SCM research for SMEs from 2003 to 2009 [33,34,35] tested only parts of the benefits. The research from Meehan and Muir [33] focuses on the benefits for SMEs, considering the barriers of adopting SCM. It could be established that SMEs in Merseyside emphasise operational and strategic benefits after implementing SCM. Fawcett et al. [34] compared very small, small and large enterprises and found that perceived achievements of the investigated benefits were not significantly different. This contradicts Arend and Wisner's [35] findings who conclude that SMEs have less strategic focus and therefore often do not reap the potential benefits of SCM, especially when they are not aligned with a larger more powerful supply chain partner.

It was found that only a limited amount of articles exist on SRM itself. No empirical research has been carried out about the benefits that may be achieved with SRM. However, some journal and magazine articles state benefits that may be achieved with the implementation of SRM [16,36,37,38].

Only one research group has carried out research about benefits of CRM in SMEs [39,40,41]. The two articles published in 2009 were based on the same primary data and therefore only the peer-reviewed journal article is considered. Harrigan et al. [39] identified and rated six benefits that may be gained by SMEs when implementing e-CRM. This, however, limits the opinion of participants, since no benefits suggestions could be made. The outcome of the article [40], shows that the level of significance has shifted for one benefit and one new benefit arose.

3.4   Summary of Results of Literature Review

Table 1 provides an overview about the previously evaluated authors that have contributed to knowledge about the benefits SMEs can achieve by introducing ES or it's components. Shading indicates that this benefit has been identified for LEs. It can be observed that a variety of potential benefits for SMEs have not been identified or not yet been researched, constituting a research need.

Table 1. Authors focusing on ES and ES component benefits for SMEs

	ES	ERP	SCM	SRM	CRM
Cost and inventory reduction	[23]	[24][25][26][28][29]	[33][34]		[39][40]
Cycle time reduction	[23]	[24][26]	[33][34]		
Productivity improvement	[23]	[24][25][27][29]	[34]		
Quality improvement		[24][26][27][28]	[33][34][35]		
Customer service improvement	[23]	[24]	[33][34][35]		[39][40]
Increased repurchases					
Increased sales by add. purchases					[40]
Increased customer lifetime value					
Better resource management	[23]	[27][28][29]			
Improved decision making, planning	[23]	[24][25][26][27]	[33]		
Performance improvement	[23]	[24][25][29]	[34]		[39][40]
Support business growth		[29]	[34][35]		
Support business alliance					
Business innovation			[33][34]		
Enabling world wide expansion					[39][40]
Enabling e-commerce		[29]	[33]		
Competitive position		[24]	[34][35]		
Improved SC effectiveness	[23]		[33][34][35]		
Increased effect of word of mouth					
Improvement of CR		[26]			[39][40]
Improvement of SR		[26]			
Enhance customer loyalty					[39][40]
Business flexibility			[34]		
IT cost reduction		[29][26]			
Increased IT infrastructure ability					
Changing work pattern	[23]	[24] - [29]			
Facilitating business learning					
Empowerment					
Building common visions					
Shifting work focus	[23]				
Increased staff moral, satisfaction					

4 Discussion

The purpose of this section is to evaluate to what extent the existing ES benefits research answers the question which benefits SMEs can expect from SaaS-based IES. First, it needs to be clarified if the difference between ES and SaaS-based IES might have any impact on the transferability of literature review findings. Second, it has to be investigated if the transferable findings are complete. This will be done by discussing findings for each ES component and finally summarizing them in a benefits framework for SaaS-based IES.

4.1   Transferability of Results

There are four main differences between all-in-one ES and SaaS-based IES. First, SaaS-based IES are hosted by specialists as vendors. Therefore, SaaS-based IESs are expected to be cheaper, easier to implement and maintain. Second, they combine all ES components in one product. This might allow higher flexibility in the choice of components compared to ES. Third, they are less complex than ES for large enterprises and are therefore easier to implement, understand, and used than alternative systems. Finally, they are accessed via Internet, which might provide more mobility, but also an additional risk of system unavailability.

Apart from these differences, SaaS-based IES offer the same functionalities as ES. Therefore the benefits for SMEs are expected to be the same. However, it has to be taken into consideration that SaaS-based IES are more affordable and therefore might be used by smaller SMEs. These might make less use of the systems, which could impact on the significance of the benefits. This phenomenon has been shown e.g. in SCM research [35]. Smaller SMEs might also have less business process transactions and therefore reap fewer benefits from business process integration. It can be summarised that the results of the literature are transferable, but need to be re-evaluated regarding their significance. They also might need to be complemented by additional benefits mentioned above.

4.2   Discussion of ES Benefits

From the identified literature only two articles were concerned with benefits of ES, one for LEs and one for SMEs. The articles outline that the majority of benefits from ERP can also be achieved with ES. Though, not all benefits identified in the literature could be establbished in SMEs. Besides that, it has to be taken into consideration that this knowledge is only based on two article with 44 and ten participants, researching industry experts and not the SMEs themselves. For SMEs the benefits were just identified and no rating was conducted. Therefore, knowledge only exists about possible benefits but not the importance of them.

4.3   Discussion of ES Components' Benefits

ERP is the best researched ES component. Even the limited SME specific research it seems to confirm that there are ERP benefits for SMEs. We compared the results with ERP research for LEs using Shang and Seddon's benefits framework [42]. Comparing various frameworks the selected one was the most comprehensive and suitable (e.g. [32,43]). The framework distinguishes between operational, managerial, strategic, IT and organizational benefits. A ranking indicates that operational benefits are most important for SMEs. In comparison to this, large enterprises put more emphasis on benefits related to strategic business development and IT [22]. It can be established that in comparison to large enterprises, SMEs were only able to take advantage of a limited amount of benefits provided by the ERP system. Existing research is mainly of qualitative nature. It would be interesting to investigate quantitative variables to get a better picture of the significance of the ERP benefits in SMEs. It has to be considered that the effect of cognitive dissonance might influence the outcome of the research.

It can be seen that the benefits achieved by LEs when implementing SCM cannot be achieved to the same extent by SMEs [34]. However, there is the tendency of achieving the same benefit groups. Since SMEs were not able to add benefits they felt were important it is questionnable if the lack of benefits is a result of non-existence or non-investigation. Furthermore, none of the organisational benefits were identified for SCM in SMEs. This might be explained by the fact that when SMEs implement SCM the aims are inter-company and not intra-company benefits and therfore no investigation aimed at those benefits.

No empirical research exists for SRM benefits, neither for LEs nor for SMEs. The findings of the literature review represent hypotheses, which SRM benefits could occur. Information of the significance of these benefits is not available.

By comparing benefits of CRM for large enterprises [18,43,44] with benefits SMEs may receive it can be seen that the main focus is very similar. Besides that, it has to be noted that according to Harrigan et al. [39,40], some benefits experienced by SMEs differ to large enterprises. It was discovered that the amount of established benefits varies significantly from large enterprises to SMEs and only a very limited empirical research exists resulting in a need for further research to confirm and possibly expand the findings.

5   A Framework for SaaS-Based Benefits for SMEs

The different results for benefits of the ES components lead to the conclusion that benefits of SaaS-based IES and their significance depend on the choice of the implementation scope. SMEs that only take advantage of intra-company functionalities (ERP) of SaaS-based IES will not be able to use the additional advantages of SCM, SRM and CRM. SMEs who only add CRM miss out on SCM/SRM benefits and their positive effects on CRM benefits. For an overview of benefits that might be achieved by selecting a certain component, Table 2 summarises potential operational benefits of IES for SMEs. For this purpose the frequency of naming as well available ratings of the findings from this literature review were taken into consideration. The significance of benefits in percentage

Table 2. Framework of potential operational benefits of SaaS-based IES in SMEs

Operational Benefits	Components							
	ERP		SCM		SRM		CRM	
	%	Rating	%	Rating	%	Rating	%	Rating
Cost and inventory reduction	68%	H	66%	M	?	?	77%	H
Cycle time reduction	58 %	M	66%	M	?	?	?	?
Productivity improvement	72%	H	33%	L	-	-	?	?
Quality improvement	72%	H	100%	H	?	?	?	?
Customer service improvement	70%	H	100%	H	?	?	80%	H

are classified as high (H), medium (M) or low (L). A question mark means that this benefit has been found for LE but has not yet been confirmed for SMEs. A dash indicates that this benefit was not found for the component.

6   Conclusions

The summary of the body of knowledge about potential benefits of ES for SMEs are useful for SMEs and researchers who are evaluating IES or just ES or components of ES for SMEs. The nature of IES for SMEs has also been clarified. It could be identified that the majority of the benefits identified in the ERP literature can be transferred to ES. However, it was discovered that the importance of benefits differs from large companies to SMEs. Furthermore, the results indicate that SMEs are not able to gain the same amount of benefits as large companies. There is still little evidence how significant these benefits are and therefore the need for more research about ES and especially for SaaS-based IES arises. It is also unclear which IT-infrastructure and organisational benefits arise.

Considering that new SaaS-based IES for SMEs are said to be as affordable as legacy systems, SMEs might benefit from implementing them. However this recommendation needs to be handled with caution, because the significance of potential benefits is still unclear. The scope of our study was limited to benefits; it excluded potential risks and disadvantages of enterprise systems. It also did not consider all potential components of SaaS-based IES. There is a lot of additional research necessary to shed more light on the evaluation of SaaS-based IES.

References

1. Markus, M.L., Tanis, S.C.: The enterprise system experience - from adoption to success. In: Zmud, R. (ed.) Framing the Domains of IT Reasearch 2000, pp. 173–207. Pinnaflex Eduaction Resources, Cincinnati (2000)
2. Weston Jr., F.: ERP II: The extended enterprise system. Business Horizons 46(6), 49–55 (2003)
3. Panorama Consulting Solutions: Clash of the titans - an independent comparison of SAP, Oracle and Microsoft Dynamics (2012), http://panorama-consulting.com/Documents/Clash-of-the-Titans-2012.pdf
4. Jacobs, R.F., Weston, F.C.T.: Enterprise resource planning (ERP) - brief history. Journal of Operations Management 25(2), 357–363 (2007)
5. Chan, J.O.: E-Business enabled ERP II Architecture. Communications of the IIMA 10(1), 11 (2010)
6. American Production and Inventory Control Society: APICS Dictionary. 10th edn. Amer Production and Inventory, United States (2001)
7. Sumner, M.: Enterprise Resource Planning. Pearson Education, Prentice Hall (2004)
8. Chen, Y., Li, X., Chen, F.: Overview and analysis of cloud computing research and application. In: International Conference on E -Business and E -Government (ICEE), Shanghai, China, pp. 1436–1439 (2011)

9. Seddon, P.B., Calvert, C., Yang, S.: A multi-project model of key factors affecting organizational benefits from enterprise systems. MIS Quarterly 34(2), 305–328 (2010)

10. Møller, C.: ERP II: a conceptual framework for next-generation enterprise systems? Journal of Enterprise Information Management 18(4), 483–497 (2005)

11. Chen, I.J., Paulraj, A.: Understanding supply chain management: critical research and a theoretical framework. International Journal of Production Research 42(1), 131–163 (2004)

12. Stadtler, H.: Supply chain management and advanced planning basics, overview and challenges. European Journal of Operational Research 163(3), 575–588 (2005)

13. Lambert, D.M., Cooper, M.C., Pagh, J.D.: Supply chain management: Implementation issues and research opportunities. International Journal of Logistics Management 9(2), 1–19 (1998)

14. Gunasekaran, A., Ngai, E.W.T.: Information systems in supply chain integration and management. European Journal of Operational Research 159(2 SPEC. ISS.), 269–295 (2004)

15. Heikkilä, J.: From supply to demand chain management. Journal of Operations Management 2, 747–767 (2002)

16. Appelfeller, W.,Buchholz, W.: Supplier relationship management - Strategie, Organisation und IT des modernen Beschaffungsmanagements. Gabler Verlag, Wiesbaden, Germany (2011)

17. Hoffmann, E., Farrell, D., Lilford, N., Ellis, M., Cant, M.: Operations and Management Principles for Contact Centres. Juta and Company, Cape Town (2008)

18. Sigala, M.: Customer relationship management (CRM) evaluation: diffusing CRM benefits into business processes. In: 13th European Conference on Information Systems, Turku, Finland, pp. 1–12 (2004)

19. Beckmann, H., Vlachakis, J., Kelkar, O., Otto, B.: Eine integrierte, offene SRM-Plattform zur Untersttzung von Beschaffungsprozessen mittelstndischer Untermehmen. HMD - Praxis der Wirtschaftsinformatik 39(228), 33–42 (2002)

20. Stölzle, W., Heusler, K.F.: Supplier Relationship Management - Entstehung, Konzeptverstndnis und methodisch-instrumentelle Anwendung. In: Bogaschewski, R., Götze, U. (eds.) Management und Controlling von Einkauf und Logistik 2003. Deutscher Betriebswirte-Verlag, Gernsbach (2003)

21. Stackpole, B.: One size doesn't always fit all. Managing Automation 22(7), 10–14 (2007)

22. Laukkanen, S., Sarpola, S., Hallikainen, P.: Enterprise size matters: objectives and constraints of ERP adoption. Journal of Enterprise Information Management 20(3), 319–334 (2007)

23. Mathrani, S., Viehland, D.: Business Benefits from Enterprise Systems Implementation in Small and Medium-sized Enterprises. Australasian Journal of Information Systems 16(1), 31–50 (2009)

24. Kale, P., Banwait, S., Laroiya, S.: Performance evaluation of ERP implementation in Indian SMEs. Journal of Manufacturing Technology Management 21(6), 758–780 (2010)

25. Federici, T.: Factors influencing ERP outcomes in SMEs: A post-introduction assessment. Journal of Enterprise Information Management 22(1-2), 81–98 (2009)

26. Mabert, V.A., Soni, A., Venkataramanan, M.A.: The impact of organization size on enterprise resource planning (ERP) implementations in the US manufacturing sector. Omega 31(3), 235–246 (2003)

27. Marsh, A.: The implementation of enterprise resource planning systems in small-medium manufacturing enterprises in South-East Queensland: a case study approach. In: International Conference on Management of Innovation and Technology, vol. 2, pp. 592–597 (2000)
28. Reuther, D.,Chattopadhyay, G.: Critical factors for enterprise resources planning system selection and implementation projects within small to medium enterprises, pp. 851–855 (2004)
29. Sedera, D., Gable, G., Chan, T.: ERP success: does organization size matter? In: 7th Pacific Asian Conference on Information Systems, pp. 1075–1088 (2003)
30. Koh, S.C.L., Gunasekaran, A., Rajkumar, D.: ERP II: The involvement, benefits and impediments of collaborative information sharing. International Journal of Production Economics 113(1), 245–268 (2008)
31. Shang, S., Seddon, P.: A comprehensive framework for classifying the benefits of ERP systems. In: 6th Americas Conference on Information Systems, Long Beach, pp. 1005–1014 (2000)
32. Wang, W., Sedera, D.: A Framework For Understanding The Benefits Of Supply Chain Management Systems. In: 15th Pacific Asia Conference on Information Systems (PACIS), Brisbane, pp. 1–12 (2011)
33. Meehan, J., Muir, L.: SCM in Merseyside SMEs: benefits and barriers. TQM Magazine 20(3), 223–232 (2008)
34. Fawcett, S.E., Allred, C., Magnan, G.M., Ogden, J.: Benchmarking the viability of SCM for entrepreneurial business model design. Benchmarking: An International Journal 16(1), 5–29 (2009)
35. Arend, R.J., Wisner, J.D.: Small business and supply chain management: is there a fit? Journal of Business Venturing 20(3), 403–436 (2005)
36. Byrne, P.M.: Maximizing value through supplier relationship management. Logistics Management 45(2), 24–25 (2006)
37. Herrmann, J., Hodgson, B.: SRM: leveraging the supply base for competitive advantage. In: SMTA International Conference, Chicago (2001)
38. Choy, K.L., Lee, W.B., Lau, H.C.W., So, S.C.K., Victor, L.: An enterprise collaborative management system: a case study of supplier selection in new product development. International Journal of Technology Management 28(2), 206–226 (2004)
39. Harrigan, P., Ramsey, E., Ibbotson, P.: e-CRM in SMEs: An exploratory study in Northern Ireland. Marketing Intelligence and Planning 26(4), 385–404 (2008)
40. Harrigan, P., Ramsey, E., Ibbotson, P.: Investigating the e-CRM activities of Irish SMEs. Journal of Small Business and Enterprise Development 16(3), 443–465 (2009)
41. Harrigan, P., Ramsey, E., Ibbotson, P.: Critical factors underpinning the e-CRM activities of SMEs. In: Conference on Market, Marketing and Entrepreneurship, Antalya, Turkey, pp. 1–37 (2009)
42. Shang, S., Seddon, P.B.: Assessing and managing the benefits of enterprise systems: the business manager's perspective. Information Systems Journal 12(4), 271–299 (2002)
43. Freeman, P., Seddon, P.B.: Benefits from CRM-based work systems. In: Proceedings European Conference on Information Systems (ECIS), Regensberg (2005)
44. Ko, E., Kim, S.H., Kim, M., Woo, J.Y.: Organizational characteristics and the CRM adoption process. Journal of Business Research 61(1), 65–74 (2008)

An Operational Planning Solution for SMEs in Collaborative and Non-Hierarchical Networks

Beatriz Andrés[1], Raúl Poler[1], and Jorge E. Hernández[2]

[1] Research Centre on Production Management and Engineering (CIGIP),
Universitat Politècnica de València (UPV)
Plaza Ferrándiz y Carbonell, 2, 03801 Alcoy, Spain
{beaanna,rpoler}@cigip.upv.es
www.cigip.org
[2] University of Liverpool Management School,
Chatham Street, Liverpool, L69 7ZH, UK
J.E.Hernandez@liverpool.ac.uk
http://www.liv.ac.uk/ulms/

Abstract. Regarding the current wide range of complexities, topologies and main characteristics linked to network environments, a large variety of collaborative network configurations can be studied and analysed. Due to the emerging importance for researchers, academia as well as practicioners, this paper focuses on collaborative and non-hierarchical networks. This type of networks are normally characterised by managing the decision-making process in a distributed manner. Hence, the exchange of information and the establishment of collaborative processes and commitments are core activities for the network partners. For this, the main orientation of this paper is, through applying the literature review method, to cover the relevant collaborative processes that SMEs need to consider when they participate in non-hierarchical networks. From the results of the literature reviewed it is determined that under the non-hierarchical network perspective, SMEs may find various difficulties to adopt collaborative processes within an optimal performance. A relevant process is the one related with the operation planning, in which this paper focuses on its collaborative perspective. In this context, and regarding the amount of agreements and standardised processes required, supporting the collaborative operational planning to produce efficient and acceptable solutions for SMEs might become one of the most complex activities to participate in collaborative non-hierarchical networks. The objective of this paper is to address the main barriers regarded the operational planning processes in non-hierarchical networks under a collaborative perspective. Moreover, a conceptual solution based on multi-agent systems is addressed, in which its application to non-hierarchical networks is analysed in order to deal with the operational planning process in collaborative and distributed environments.

Keywords: non-hierarchical networks, collaborative processes, distributed decision making, operational planning process, SMEs.

J.E. Hernández et al. (Eds.): EWG-DSS 2012, LNBIP 164, pp. 46–56, 2013.
© Springer-Verlag Berlin Heidelberg 2013

1   Introduction

A growing number of organisational forms in collaborative networks are emerging as a result of the information and communication technologies (ICT) advances, the market and society needs and the research progress to cope the main enterprise collaboration issues. In addition, from a decision support system perspective, it is established that an effective collaboration leads to collaborative advantages and also to a better partnership performance [15]. Moreover, issues such as the increase of competitiveness, customer requirements, the use of dispersed knowledge, the need to address global-scale issues and the globalisation requires SMEs joint efforts and global collaboration [23].

As defined in [14], [18], from a network information flow perspective, collaborative processes in traditional hierarchical networks (HN) or non-hierarchical networks (NHN) might be seen from a centralized or decentralized perspective. On the one hand, in the centralized perspective, typically addressed to NH, the information flows around one central node to support the decision-making process of the whole network. On the other hand, the decentralized perspective, typically addressed to NHN, is characterised in that every firm in the network carries out its own decision-making process independently. Hence, a decentralised perspective in front of a centralised one will be more realistic in current networks, especially for those consisting of SMEs [2]. In this decentralized context, the decision-making process might be optimized by also considering the different decisional levels and the individual goals of each network nodes. Thereafter, and in light of this NHN in which all the networked partners are involved in the business processes management, decisions on decentralised models (DDM) will generally consider multi-level and multi-directional information flow among partners in a collaborative and committed way [27].

From the aforementioned premises, the contribution of this paper is to present the results from the reviewed literature in which it has been obtained an overview of the most relevant collaborative processes SMEs have to consider to perform their activities in order to, first, overcome the needs they could have when collaborative processes in non-hierarchical networks are carried out and, second, to support their decisions based on decentralised models. Amongst all the processes identified in the literature review, in which the network partners are collaboratively involved, the operational planning process is particularly studied. Furthermore, and considering the previous research from [3], [4], this paper analyses how the novel *Supply Chain Agent-based Modelling Methodology that supports a Collaborative Planning Approach* (SCAMM-CPA) approach [14], [16], [18] adapts to the non-hierarchical scenario to collaboratively deal with the operational planning process from a decentralised perspective.

2   SMEs Collaborative Processes in NHN

SMEs nature and *modus operandi* is evolving towards establishing partnerships with other companies, in complex value chains, that are led to perform decentralised decisions in order to support their management activities. The establishment of DDM, the need for establishing collaborative mechanisms and the need to exchange only public information reveals a set of SMEs needs and barriers that must be overcame in order to efficiently participate in collaborative NHNs. As a result of this, it can be stated that collaborative processes have associated a number of problems and issues that must be supported in order to properly perform a collaborative environment in NHNs. These problems appear due to the fact that the establishment of collaborative processes requires: a great exchange of information and communication amongst the participant nodes, the consideration of public and private information management, the SMEs readiness to adopt DDM and the SMEs preparation to deal with the establishment of collaborative processes.

Hence, and by considering the previous work from [3, 4], the most relevant processes that SMEs adopt to support collaborative relationships in a decentralised environment are shown in Table 1. From this, Table 1 reveals the existence of many collaborative processes affecting inter-enterprise collaboration for which some models (M), guidelines (G) and tools (T) are provided as a collection of solutions to support collaborative processes [3]. Moreover, the identified collaborative processes are conceptually arranged according to the strategic (S), tactical (T) and operational (O) decision levels. This classification can be seen as helpful to support researchers devoted to assist SMEs in order to overcome the problems and needs associated with their participation in collaborative NHN. In addition, Table 1 provides a classification scheme for the processes by which the SMEs are influenced when they decide to participate in collaborative networks, from both the HN and NHN perspective.

Despite the fact that processes are considered from the collaborative point of view, it is important to highlight that, in the literature reviewed by [3], most of identified processes are discussed and addressed form centralised approaches (HN perspective) instead of decentralised approaches that characterises NHN.

In light of this, the *degree of coverage* criteria is defined to identify in each collaborative process, determined by [3, 4], the extent to which the process is treated, in the literature, considering the decentralised perspective (NHN). The degree of coverage for each collaborative process can be seen in table 1.

In this way, if the process is addressed from the decentralised perspective it is possible to say that the degree of coverage is excellent (●) due to the treatment done in the literature for a specific process is set out to support the NHN context.

On the other hand, if the process is treated considering the features of centralised approaches (HN perspective), then it must be determined into which extent the processes are discussed in the literature from the NHN view. Regarding to this, table 2 provides a classification and notation to identify the degree of coverage of each collaborative process: poor (○), unsatisfactory (◔), acceptable (◑) or satisfactory (◕).

Table 1. Collaborative Processes Classification - adapted from [3]

Models		
Guidelines		
Tools		

Strategic		Tactical		Operational	
(1) Network Design	◗	(1) Forecast Demand	◗	(1) Scheduling	◗
(2) Decision System Design	◗	(2) Operational Planning	◗	(2) OPP	◗
(3) Partners Selection	◗	(3) Replenishment	◗	(3) Lotsizing Negotiation	◖
(4) Strategy Alignment	◖	(4) Performance Management	◗	(4) Inventory Management.	◗
(5) Partners Coordination	◗	(5) Knowledge Management.	◗	(5) Information Exchange	◗
(6) Product Design	◗	(6) Uncertainty Management.	◗	(6) Process Connection	◗
(7) PMS Design	◗	(7) Negotiation Contracts among partners	◗	(7) Interoperability	◗
(8) Coordination Mechanisms Design	◗	(8) Share costs/profits	◖		
		(9) Coordination Mechanisms Management	◗		

Collaborative Processes

Table 2. Solutions Degree of Coverage - adapted from [3]

Degree of coverage		Description
Poor	○	The process is only addressed from the centralised perspective, what characterises HN
Unsatisfactory	◔	The process is addressed in the literature through considering concepts or ideas that can be implemented in the decentralised perspective, but the approaches treating the process cannot be applied to NHN due to are subject to HN features
Acceptable	◑	The process is treated and addressed for HN scenarios but the approaches to address the process can be applied, through adaptations, to NHN
Satisfactory	◕	The process is treated from different perspectives, centralised and decentralised, but the predominance perspective is the decentralised, therefore most of approaches to address the process can be adapted or are defined for NHN
Excellent	●	The process is treated, addressed and discussed from the decentralised perspective, NHN context

3   The Operational Planning Process

Amongst the collaborative processes identified in Table 1 to deal with the SMEs participation in collaborative NHN, based on the DDM, the operational planning process, classified at the tactical decision level, is selected regarding to its relevance for establishing collaborative relations among networked partners. At this decisional level, as studied in [14], [16], [18], collaborative approaches imply the information sharing in terms of planning process oriented to support the implementation and evaluation of joint activity programs to achieve common goals. This means sharing information in terms of risks, resources, responsibilities and rewards, for instance. Hence, collaboration can be seen as the mutual participants' commitment to jointly solve problems.

Operational planning, such as production, inventory management and distribution processes, is a key factor in network management. Given the complex management of the network and the different goal-based objectives among partners, it is desirable to develop scenarios to integrate all the nodes through the network planning [13]. Hence, the collaborative planning is defined as an interactive process in which partners continuously collaborate and share demand information to jointly plan their activities [31] and might be seen from a centralised or decentralised perspective.

3.1   Operational Planning Solutions

Given the complex management linked to NHN environments and to the potential contradictory objectives that might emerge among partners due to its nature, it is desirable to develop a scenario to integrate all the nodes; this is possible through the operational planning process [13]. The main idea, to be applied in NHN, is to extend the planning process, initially local, towards different planning domains [30], to get a beneficial plan for everyone, based on mutual agreements.

As aforesaid, the collaborative planning process can be considered as centralised or decentralized; NHN are characterised by decentralised scenarios, where each node is responsible for exchanging its own information and making its own decisions. Collaborative and decentralised planning involves all the partners and takes into account the objectives and constraints from all the nodes in the NHN. Thereafter, a decentralised approach like this will require coordination mechanisms, pre-agreed business rules, evaluation and comparison of alternatives using performance measures [12], in order to support the operational planning [31].

Four key factors are considered to address decentralised collaborative planning [30]: (i) the mediator, (ii) the initial solution, (iii) the number of exchanged offers and (iv) the expected final results. As previously stated, a set of models, guidelines and tools are given by [3] as a collection of solutions to support collaborative processes, thus the operational planning solutions are also provided regarding this classification.

Models that address the planning process according to the type of decision-making can be centralised [9], partially centralised [22] or decentralised [7]. To address the collaborative and decentralised planning process, a multi-objective planning model under uncertainty (in demand, materials, etc.) can be adopted by the NHN decision units [13], [25]. Fuzzy Goal Programming (FGP) is also a potential decentralised approach to solve collaborative planning models [28]. In this way, decentralised decision-making plans among members can be synchronised and aligned using non-hierarchical negotiations based on compensation schemes [11], [14], [16], [18]; an application of this is the collaborative planning scheme consisting of two phases to improve the planning results: the top-down planning [5], and the negotiation scheme. Another application of non-hierarchical negotiation is A Decentralised Supply Chain Planning methodology (ADSCP) which allows partners to create network plans by the simple exchange of information on the supply quantities [19].

Guidelines provided in the literature are proposed from a decentralised perspective allowing decision makers to use them as a support to collaborative planning in NHN. Guidelines to model the operational planning process allows decision makers to identify and structure the information and influential issues, affecting collaborative planning, in a single diagram [17], [21]. To enhance collaboration in planning, a number of methodologies are available such as Operations Planning and Sequencing methodology (OPS), based on IE-GIP and GRAI [24], which allows the decision makers to improve the network planning by increasing collaboration through DGRAI tool [20]. Furthermore it is available the COC PLAN TOOL (Collaboration Opportunity Characterisation & VO Rough Planning) to support the collaborative planning by mapping different collaboration areas [8].

From the tools point of view, the operational planning management process commonly uses agent-based approaches, such as Multi-Agent Supply Chain Coordination Tool (MASCOT) [26], Multi-Agent System for collaborative production planning (MASCOPP), which lets decision makers to synchronise decentralised production plans [10] and the Supply Chain Agent-based Modelling Methodology that supports a Collaborative Planning Approach (SCAMM-CPA) to support the collaborative planning modelling process in the network [14], [16]. Besides, several projects agent-based have been carried out to solve the production planning problem [29].

Summing-up, in the context of the operational planning, solutions for collaborative processes are collected, both in HN and NHN context. Table 3 illustrates a classification scheme from the literature reviewed in [3], and above briefly explained, on collaborative operational planning solutions, taking into account the classification scheme based on the type of provided solutions (models – M, guidelines – G and tools – T).

Table 3. Operational Planning Solutions

Operational Planning Solutions	**MODELS**: planning domains [30], decentralised planning, Partially centralised SCMP [22], SC Planning matrix, APS [31], e-constraint method [25], planning models under uncertainty [23], network decentralised planning [31, 7], Fuzzy Goal Programming [28], conceptual modelling of planning processes [17]
	GUIDELINES: iterative collaborative planning [12], non-hierarchical negotiations based on compensation schemes [11], ADSCP, Decentralised supply chain planning framework (Jung et al., 2008), interoperability [1], OPS [20] , Collaborative solutions for decision-making [15]
	TOOLS: ACI [6], SCAMM-CPA [14], [16], [18], MASCOPP [10], MASCOT [26], eXPlanTech, ProPlanT [29], DGRAI [20] ,[24] COC PLAN TOOL [8]

3.2   Application of the Agent-Based Methodology SCAMM-CPA to Support the SMEs Collaborative Planning in NHN

Multi-agent systems (MAS) is a robust tool to deal with the decision-making, information flown and simulation modelling process, especially in networked environments. MAS are recognised to support the model complex configuration of networks [16]. This tool is commonly used to overcome the operational planning management process in networks [10], [16], [26]. Some well-know examples about using agents to support collaborative environments are: MASCOT [26] - *Multi-Agent Supply Chain Coordination Tool*, MASCOPP [10] - *Multi-Agent System for collaborative production planning* -, which supports the synchronisation of decentralised production plans and SCAMM-CPA methodology [16], [18] -*Supply Chain Agent-based Modelling Methodology that supports a Collaborative Planning Approach*-, which is mainly oriented to support the collaborative planning process in supply chain network.

Amongst all the identified solutions, the novel SCAMM-CPA approach is considered particularly interesting to support the decentralised decisions in networks due to its collaborative decision-making agent-based model/application. The SCAMM-CPA approach, extended by [18] for more complex and generic environments, is oriented to support the design and implementation of the most important collaborative network processes, such as forecasting, order management, production planning, replenishment and product-distribution by considering a novel implementation of collaborative mechanisms among companies based on distributed agents. From the extension of [16] to [18], a novel structured architecture has been generated over the standard perspectives and dimensions of the *Zachman Framework* [32] in which the main data, functions, people, motivations, temporal and spatial relationship are identified and defined. The main purpose of the proposed architecture is the information flow that support interoperability among the networked nodes and the decision-making process related to each node. In this sense, it is possible to say that collaboration involves many types of processes, and [16, 18] propose an interoperable architecture to support the collaborative planning within networks.

Although, SCAMM-CPA is validated by applying it to an automotive supply chain the SCAMM-CPA architecture implements a MAS-based tool to support any supply chain topology. The architecture has been generated in order to be as generic as possible to make it adaptable to any type of network. Regarding to this, it is possible to support the design and implementation of the collaborative network planning process, particularly in NHN. Specifically in the NHN context, the tool is to be installed in each network node in order to provide an automated system to negotiate demand plans between any pair of network nodes, enabling the consideration of restrictions in all the nodes involved to generate an efficient response to the network's customer demand. Hence, NHN are to be implemented by considering the networked nodes behaviours and decision-making mechanisms from the collaborative and decentralised perspective. Therefore, the SCAMM-CPA is considered an innovative research solution to deal with collaborative planning in NHN.

The SCAMM-CPA methodology consist of nine phases that can be applied to NHN in order to solve the collaborative operational planning problem: problem identification (A), problem conceptualisation (B), parameterisation (C), main agents identification (D), analysis of interdependence relationship among agents: identification of intermediate agents (E), behaviour representation among agents (F), conceptual agent-based model (G), development of the agent-based application (H) and validation (I).

The SCAMM-CPA approach is provided with six layers, table 4 shows how each layer from the SCAMM-CPA can be adapted from a NHN viewpoint, relating the collaborative and decentralised characteristics of the NHN with SCAMM-CPA and adapting each layer to the NHN features.

Accordingly, from Table 4, SCAMM-CPA methodology provides a collaboration layer established for every node from an independent perspective considering common information oriented to support the collaborative planning in networks and making it useful to be considered in SMEs environments; making it accessible from the decentralised nodes and getting closer the collaborative NHN point of view. Thus, with SCAMM-CPA, the relationship among the collaborative nodes is supported by the demand plan exchanging process, which will collaboratively promote the negotiation of unfeasible values overcoming the barriers associated with collaborative planning process among NHN partners.

Table 4. Application of SCAMM-CPA to non-hierarchical networks (NHN) [16]

SCAMM-CPA LAYERS	NHN - Solution application
❶ Physical Layer	Through this layer the NHN configuration is analysed as well as the resources and items related to it. This layer provide aspects like the enterprise flows and topologies in which can be included NHN. This is also considered as the real system in where the decision making process take places among the NHN partners. This layer allows considering any kind of network configuration.
❷ Data Layer	This layer is considered as a repository of systems providing simplified access to stored data by considering an entity relational database regarding the NHN. From a decentralised point of view, every node in the NHN considers its own data base. This layer defines the main data structure.
❸ Information Layer	The information layer collects, manage and structure all the necessary information for the information exchange process from a generically view in order to support the upper layer on the collaborative processes within the NHN. This layer allows the treatment of all the necessary information to support collaborative processes within the networked partners.
❹ Ontology REA-based Layer	In this case, the REA enterprise ontology is considered regarding to its standard approach and to its simplicity in the modelling process within complex NHN. Thus, at this layer the description logic is established by considering economical resources, events and multi-agent systems. After this, in order to support the connectivity with the MAS (layer ❺) a semantic language is chosen in order to support the communication between the physical and agent layer. This layer can be supported by some ontological software designer, such as *Protégé* for supporting standards communication processes in collaborative NHN.
❺ Agent Communication Layer	This layer is oriented to support the MAS infrastructure in order to provide the information requested among the networked partners. Thus, the information flows consider aspects such as the transfer and processing of the information which is linked to the corresponding database of the NHN nodes. *JADE* is proposed as the most common library which supports the decentralised structure of NHN. Therefore, this layer implements the mechanism for the decentralised decision-making what characterises NHN.
❻ Behaviour Layer	The behaviour layer can be defined in three types, the first one related to MAS which generates a *call for proposal ACL message* (CFP) offers and receive proposals or inform in a ACL language, the second one related to the reception of CFP and proposal and the generation of CFP messages as well, and the last one oriented to receive the CFP request and answer by accepting, refusing or proposing the CFP request. The behaviour layer collects the basic structure of the NHN.

4   Conclusions

This paper gives for the community researchers an insight of the most relevant collaborative processes. Collaborative processes in NHN are to be implemented by considering own behaviours and decision-making mechanisms in a collaborative and decentralised perspective. The literature review reveals the existence of a set of collaborative processes which most of them are treated from the HN context. In order to manage this, the degree of coverage criteria is proposed so as to determine for each collaborative process the extent to which it is treated and discussed from the NHN context.

The research objective in this paper is to achieve a better understanding of the ways how SME's address collaborative problems. Amongst the relevant collaborative processes that affect the establishment of collaborative relationships within a network this paper particularly addresses the operational planning process. Within the operational planning arena, different works are identified in the literature reviewed, providing solutions in the NHN context. In light of this, MAS are considered as appropriate approaches to model collaborative processes from a decentralised perspective, in which the information coming from the collaborative and non-collaborative networked nodes must be identified.

To deal with the operational planning problem a solution based on the SCAMM-CPA is analysed to determine the applicability considering the collaborative and decentralised features in NHN. This novel approach is considered as a potential methodology to solve the operational planning among NHN partners due to the 6 layers in which the SCAMM-CPA consists of are all applicable to the NHN context.

Future research lines are first focused on modelling the NHN characteristics in the novel methodology SCAMM-CPA due to it has been made evident that this approach can be implemented form the NHN point of view.

Although many works treat collaborative processes, very few studies exist on non-hierarchical network topologies. Therefore, the second aim of the future research is to continuing looking for new solutions for developing a framework for non-hierarchical manufacturing networks in collaborative environments that will focus on processes which current literature do not provide satisfactory degrees of coverage in NHN context. As it has been provided in the table 1 of section 2, many collaborative processes need to be further studied form the NHN perspective, that is, considering the processes treatment from the decentralised decision making view to overcome possible barriers SMEs can find in the establishment of collaborative relationships within the same network.

The goal will be to achieve a better understanding about how SMEs deal with problems related to the establishment of collaborative processes, specifically in NHN. Hence, an additional future work will be oriented to provide models, guidelines and tools for supporting collaborative processes, specifically in the NHN context aligned with SMEs requirements in manufacturing environments.

Once the most relevant processes in collaborative network environment have been identified this paper considers achieving a better understanding on how SMEs face collaboration and their barriers associated in NHN. Further research directions for wider audience are based on considering the processes treated form the HN perspective, those with poor, unsatisfactory or acceptable degrees of coverage in order to, depending on their arena of research, provide solutions, in the shape of models, guidelines and tools to overcame this problems and embed in SMEs a more willing behaviour regarding collaboration considering the premise that collaborative processes can be easily applied.

References

1. Alemany, M.E., Alarcón, F., Lario, F.C., Poler, R.: Conceptual framework for the interoperability requirements of collaborative planning process. In: Popplewell, K., Harding, J., Ricardo, C., Poler, R. (eds.) Enterprise Interoperability IV. Making the Internet of the Future for the Future of Enterprise, pp. 25–34. Springer (2010)
2. Alemany, M.M.E., Alarcón, F., Lario, F.-C., Boj, J.J.: An application to support the temporal and spatial distributed decision-making process in supply chain collaborative planning. Computers in Industry 62, 519–540 (2011)
3. Andrés, B., Poler, R.: Análisis de los Procesos Colaborativos en Redes de Empresas No-Jerárquicas. In: Ros, L., Fuente, M.V., Hontoria, E., Soler, M.D., Morales, C., Bogataj, M. (eds.) V Congreso de Ingeniería de Organización, Cartagena, pp. 369–373 (2011)

4. Andrés, B., Poler, R.: Relevant Problems in Collaborative Processes of Non-Hierarchical Manufacturing Networks. In: Prado, J.C., García, J., Comesaña, J.A., Fernández, A.J. (eds.) 6th International Conference on Industrial Engineering and Industrial Management, Vigo, Spain, July 18-20, pp. 90–97 (2012)
5. Biennier, F., Aubry, R., Maranzana, M.: Integration of business and industrial knowledge on services to set trusted business communities of organisations. In: Camarinha-Matos, L.M., Boucher, X., Afsarmanesh, H. (eds.) PRO-VE 2010. IFIP AICT, vol. 336, pp. 420–426. Springer, Heidelberg (2010)
6. Bonfatti, F., Martinelli, L., Monari, P.D.: Autonomic approach to planning and scheduling in networked small factories. In: Camarinha-Matos, L.M., Boucher, X., Afsarmanesh, H. (eds.) PRO-VE 2010. IFIP AICT, vol. 336, pp. 297–303. Springer, Heidelberg (2010)
7. Caliusco, M.L., Villarreal, P.: Decentralized management model of a partner to partner collaborative relationship. In: Second World Conference on POM and 15th Annual POM Conference, Cancun, pp. 1–31 (2004)
8. Camarinha-Matos, L.M., Oliveira, A.I., Demsar, D., Sesana, M., Molina, A., Baldo, F.: VO creation assistance services. In: Camarinha-Matos, L., Afsarmanesh, H., Ollus, M. (eds.) Methods and Tools for Collaborative Networked Organizations, pp. 155–190. Computer Science Springer (2008)
9. Chen, C.L., Wang, B.W., Lee, W.C.: Multiobjective Optimization for a Multienterprise Supply Chain Network. Industrial & Engineering Chemistry Research 42, 1879–1889 (2003)
10. Dangelmaier, W., Heidenreich, J., Pape, U.: Supply chain management: A multi-agent system for collaborative production planning. In: International Conference on e-Technology, e-Commerce and e-Service, Hong Kong, pp. 309–314 (2005)
11. Dudek, G., Stadtler, H.: Negotiation-based collaborative planning between supply chains partners. European Journal of Operational Research 163, 668–687 (2005)
12. Goetschalckx, M., Rleischmann, B.: Strategic network planning. In: Stadtler, H., Kilger, C. (eds.) Supply Chain Management and Advanced Planning, pp. 117–137 (2005)
13. Gupta, A., Maranas, C.D.: Managing demand uncertainty in supply chain planning. Computers & Chemical Engineering 27, 1219–1227 (2003)
14. Hernández, J.E., Mula, J., Poler, R., Lyons, A.C.: A decentralised and collaborative supply chain planning model supported by a multiagent-based negotiation approach. Group Decision and Negotiation (in press, 2013)
15. Hernández, J.E., Zarate, P., Dargam, F., Delibašić, B., Liu, S., Ribeiro, R. (eds.): EWG-DSS 2011. LNBIP, vol. 121. Springer, Heidelberg (2012)
16. Hernández, J.E., Alemany, M.M.E., Lario, F.C., Poler, R.: SCAMM-CPA: A supply chain agent-based modelling methodology that supports a collaborative planning process. INNOVAR 19, 99–120 (2009)
17. Hernández, J.E., Mula, J., Ferriols, F.J.: A reference model for conceptual modelling of production planning processes. Production Planning & Control 19, 725–734 (2008)
18. Hernández, J.E.: Propuesta de una arquitectura para el soporte de la planificación de la producción colaborativa en cadenas de suministro de tipo árbol. PhD Thesis (2011)
19. Jung, H., Frank Chen, F., Jeong, B.: Decentralized supply chain planning framework for third party logistics partnership. Computers & Industrial Engineering 55, 348–364 (2008)
20. Lario, F.C., Ortiz, A., Poler, R., Perez, D.: Supply chain management. In: IEEE Conference on Modelling Collaborative Decision. Emerging Technologies and Factory Automation, vol. 2, pp. 137–141 (2003)

21. Pérez, D., Alemany, M.M.E., Lario, F.C., Hernandez, J.E.: Framework for Modelling the Decision View of the Supply Chains Collaborative Planning Process. International Journal of Decision Support System Technology 4, 59–77 (2012)
22. Pibernik, R., Sucky, E.: An approach to inter-domain master planning in supply chains. International Journal of Production Economics 108, 200–212 (2007)
23. Poler, R., Carneiro, L.M., Jasinski, T., Zolgahadri, M., Pedrazzoli, P.: Intelligent Non-hierarchical Manufacturing Networks. ISTE-Willey (2013)
24. Poler, R., Lario, F.C., Doumeingts, G.: Dynamic modelling of decision systems (DMDS). Computers in Industry 49, 175–193 (2002)
25. Sabri, E.H., Beamon, B.M.: A multi-objective approach to simultaneous strategic and operational planning in supply chain design. International Journal of Management Science 28, 581–598 (2000)
26. Sadeh, N.M., Hildum, D.W., Kjenstad, D., Tseng, A.: MASCOT: An agent-based architecture for dynamic supply chain creation and coordination in the internet economy. Production Planning & Control 12, 212–223 (2001)
27. Schneeweiss, C.: Distributed decision making - a unified approach. European Journal of Operational Research 150, 237–252 (2003)
28. Selim, H., Araz, C., Ozkarahan, I.: Collaborative production–distribution planning in supply chain: A fuzzy goal programming approach. Transportation Research Part E: Logistics and Transportation Review 44, 396–419 (2008)
29. Shen, W., Hao, Q., Yoon, H.J., Norrie, D.H.: Applications of agent-based systems in intelligent manufacturing: An updated review. Advanced Engineering Informatics 20, 415–431 (2006)
30. Stadtler, H., Kilger, C.: Supply chain management and advanced planning-concepts, models, Software and Case Studies. Springer, Berlin (2002)
31. Stadtler, H.: A framework for collaborative planning and state-of-the-art. Or Spectrum 31, 5–30 (2009)
32. Zachman, J.: A Framework for Information Systems Architecture. IBM Systems Journal 26, 276–292 (1987)

On the Application of AHP to the Diagnostic
of Portuguese SME

Bruno Gonçalo Nunes[1], João Paulo Costa[1,2], and Pedro Godinho[1,3]

[1] Faculdade de Economia, Universidade de Coimbra
Av. Dias da Silva, n° 165, 3004-512 Coimbra, Portugal
[2] INstituto de Engenharia de Sistemas e Computadores de Coimbra (INESC – Coimbra)
[3] Grupo de Estudos Monetários e Financeiros (GEMF)
bgnn@live.com.pt, {jpaulo,pgodinho}@fe.uc.pt

Abstract. In this paper we present an application of the Analytic Hierarchy Process (AHP) to evaluate intervention measures in Portuguese Small and Medium-sized Enterprises (SMEs). These intervention measures result from an external diagnostic performed under the QREN program ("Quadro de Referência Estratégico Nacional" – National Strategic Reference Framework). QREN aims at the development of Portuguese economy and is financed by the European Union. The AHP application enables to acquire more knowledge about the decision process, to rank the intervention measures and to focus on the most promising ones. We consider different ways of applying AHP to rank of intervention measures, and we argue that the classical use of AHP is not the most appropriate for the type of application at hand. We present the results of applying the AHP to two cases. The results show that this application adds consistency and focus to the interventions in the framework of QREN.

Keywords: AHP – Analytic Hierarchy Process, SME – Small and Medium-sized Enterprises, National Strategic Reference Framework, Intervention Measures.

1   Introduction

The QREN program ("Quadro de Referência Estratégico Nacional" – National Strategic Reference Framework) aims at developing the Portuguese economy and is financed by the European Union. The AEP ("Associação Empresarial de Portugal" – Portuguese Business Association) is the organization bearing management responsibilities within this framework. For this matter, the AEP developed a guidebook ("Manual de Organização e Funcionamento" – MOF – [1]) structuring and guiding the application of economic and management measures, taking into account a set of specific requirements and constraints imposed by the European Union.

Although being the most common type of enterprise in Portugal, Small and Medium Enterprises (SMEs) (enterprises with less than 100 employees) are plagued by several types of problems: lack of management skills, poor market positioning, low quality control, absence of marketing plans, low productivity and poor motivation among their employees [2]. This situation occurs on all type of SMEs independently of being from the services, industry or agriculture sectors.

J.E. Hernández et al. (Eds.): EWG-DSS 2012, LNBIP 164, pp. 57–71, 2013.
© Springer-Verlag Berlin Heidelberg 2013

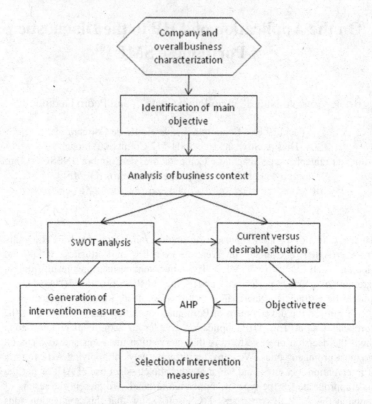

Fig. 1. The proposed SME diagnostic process

The project FPME ("Formação Pequenas e Médias Empresas" – Vocational Training for SMEs) is encompassed by the QREN framework and aims at enhancing SMEs performance through the improvement of management quality, the introduction of new organizational structures and technology, the access to new markets and the incorporation of social responsibility [1] independently of the sector of activity. This project follows a training-action philosophy in which (external) consultants develop their activity around the following vectors: company diagnostic, suggestion of intervention measures and training of the company collaborators (including entrepreneurs). According to the MOF [1] the diagnostic must encompass:

- the characterization of both company and overall business;
- the identification of objectives;
- the analysis of the business context;
- a SWOT (Strengths, Weaknesses, Opportunities, and Threats) analysis;
- a comparison of the current situation with the desirable situation;
- a hierarchical structure (a tree) of goals (objectives).

Using the objective tree, consultants and management staff identify, propose and develop a set of intervention measures (actions) and define the corresponding training plan. By including the social responsibility component, a strategic plan of medium-long term is concluded.

The set of proposed measures usually includes more measures than the ones that can be funded, and it is often impractical to undertake all the chosen measures at the same time. So it is important to evaluate and rank the proposed measures in order to choose the ones that should be undertaken, and also to schedule their application. We suggest the use of the Analytic Hierarchy Process (AHP), as defined by Saaty [3], in order to evaluate the intervention measures according to the objective tree (Fig. 1). This way, AHP is a complement to the process defined in [1], allowing us to rank the intervention measures and to focus on the most promising ones for funding and for earlier implementation. As a byproduct of this evaluation, the consistency of the objective tree is also tested and the hierarchical structure of goals can be rebuilt in case of inconsistency.

In fact, we intend AHP to be used as an aid for the decision-makers to better understand the consequences of the chosen measures, and not as a way of black-boxing this choice. AHP is one of the most used methods in multicriteria decision making and is used in several approaches for increasing the knowledge of the decision-making process – for example, it is the operational support of the cognitive constructivism considered in the multicriteria procedural rationality paradigm ([4], [5]). The idea that underlies the approach we followed is that the AHP results will not be automatically applied, but will instead be analysed by the decision-makers, in order to assess whether they are sensible. This way, AHP will let decision-makers increase their knowledge about the available alternatives and about the decision process, and will also help them choose the alternatives in which they should focus, but will not replace their judgment.

When searching the internet to find suitable software for AHP implementation, we found a large amount of possibilities. We selected a small number of implementations, ranging from simple Microsoft Excel templates to more sophisticated systems, and used them in SMEs diagnostic cases. Two of them were specially preferred by the users: a Microsoft Excel template (http://bpmsg.com/) and the system "Make it Rational" (https://makeitrational.com/). The users are the consultants and the SMEs management staff responsible for the development of the SME diagnostic. These software applications had the benefit of being affordable and user-friendly. In fact, many users preferred to use an Excel template that would allow them to use a spreadsheet they were already familiar with than to learn to use a new interface.

In this paper we discuss the application of AHP to acquire knowledge about the decision process and to rank the intervention measures. We start by briefly presenting AHP and discussing some difficulties in its application to the evaluation of these intervention measures. We argue that the classical use of AHP is not the most appropriate for this type of application. Then we present the results of applying AHP to two cases. The results show that this application adds consistency and focus to the interventions of the FPME in the framework of QREN. Finally, we will give some clues to future work on developing a support system not only for the application of AHP but also for supporting the selection of intervention measures according to the current situation found in an SME.

2   The AHP Method

2.1   Brief Presentation of the AHP Method

The AHP is a multi-criteria decision support method initially developed by Saaty [3]. The AHP starts by structuring the decision problem, according to a hierarchy of objectives and sub-objectives (or criteria and subcriteria): a tree of objectives. The sub-objectives of each level (or children) are pair-wise compared, according to their predecessor (or parent). Several different scales have been proposed for the pairwise comparisons [6], the most usual being the scale proposed by Saaty [7]. This scale uses integer numbers from 1 to 9 and their reciprocals.

A matrix of pair-wise comparisons is built and used to compute the impact, or importance, weights of each sub-objective on their predecessors. Several different methods have been proposed for the calculation of priorities, but none seems to offer a clear improvement over the original method proposed by Saaty (see, e.g., [6]). According to this method, the priority vector is based on the principal right eigenvector of the comparison matrix [7]. In order to obtain the priority vector, this eigenvector may be normalized in two different ways. The first one corresponds to the most common mode of application of the AHP, the "distributive mode", and consists on normalizing the eigenvector so that the sum of the priorities is one. The second one corresponds to the "ideal mode" of the AHP, and consists on normalizing the eigenvector so that the largest priority is one.

The evaluation of the alternatives follows the same process. In order to compute the impact weights of the alternatives on the main objective (the root of the tree), the obtained weights in each path from the main objective to the alternative, are multiplied. After that, the path values that correspond to the same alternative are added.

Some degree of inconsistency is expected among pair-wise comparisons of the elements (objectives or alternatives), mostly due to some possible intransitivity. If A is 3 times more important than B and if B is 3 times more important than C, for instance, it is expected that A is 9 times more important than C. If A is judged to be 7 times more important than C, then there will be some degree of intransitivity. Saaty [7] proposes to measure that inconsistency using a ratio (the consistency ratio – CR) which results from dividing the normalized difference between the maximum eigenvalue of the matrix and the number of rows (and columns) of the matrix (in a consistent matrix this eigenvalue is equal to the number of rows and columns) by the average normalized difference found in matrixes randomly generated. Godinho et al. [8] provide a detailed description of the application of the AHP.

2.2   Some Issues about the Application of AHP to the Intervention Measures

The AHP is a well-known and accepted method, though it also presents some application problems:

- the choice of the pairwise comparison scale and of the method for calculating the priorities;
- rank reversal – in some cases (usually by misuse) it is possible that the rank of existing alternatives is changed when an irrelevant alternative is added;
- difficulties in comparing three or more very different elements – in some cases we can have, for instance, that A is 9 times more important than B and that B is 9 times more important than C, so A should 81 times more important than C;
- a large number of comparisons to be made – if, for instance, we have to rank 10 alternatives we will have 90 pair-wise comparisons for each objective in the lower level.

Regarding the pairwise comparison scale, we chose the scale originally proposed by Saaty [3] (the usual scale that uses 1-9 and reciprocals). This is an intuitive and simple scale. However, some authors (Bana e Costa and Vansnicke [9], Barzilai [10]) argue that a ratio scale should not be used, because there are cases where the absolute zero does not make sense. These authors propose the use of ratios of differences instead. Other authors propose other scales, namely: Harker and Vargas [11] present a quadratic scale; Lootsma [12] presents a geometric scale; Salo and Hämäläinen [13] propose a balanced scale so that the weights of the alternatives/criteria are in the range of [0.1, 0.9], in order to give more sensitivity to the scale when comparing similar alternatives; Ma and Zheng [14] put forward two scales where linearity can be found on the inverse of the values instead of on the direct values. Beynon [15] and Dong et al. [6] attempt to compare several of these scales considering different cases and frameworks. They found that each scale should be used with a proper (and different) method for calculating the priority vector. In regard to this method, and considering that we chose the original scale, we chose the usual principal right eigenvector. The choice of the best scale is difficult and authors like Harker and Vargas [11] and Ishizaka and Labib [16] argue that this choice depends on the involved people and on the decision problem.

Another important decision concerns the choice of the synthesis mode: whether to use the ideal or the distributive mode. Millet and Saaty [17] propose guidelines for the choice of a synthesis mode. According to the authors, the choice should take into account whether it is more important the extent to which an alternative dominates all other alternatives under a criterion or how well each alternative performs relative to a fixed benchmark. In the former case the authors recommend the distributive mode and, in the latter, the ideal mode. The authors propose the following test for the use of the distributive mode: "if the decision maker indicates that the preference for a top ranked alternative under a given criterion would improve if the performance of any lower ranked alternative was adjusted downward, then you should use the distributive synthesis mode" ([17], p. 208).

In the case of the type of application presented in this paper, it was considered that the existence of a smaller number of alternatives for improving a given objective would make the top ranked alternative more valuable. This meant that the distributive mode was considered more appropriate, and was therefore chosen.

An issue causing some discomfort about the use of AHP is the so called 'rank reversal', that is the possibility of the change of the ranking of existing alternatives when one irrelevant alternative is added. This is due to the relative evaluation of the alternatives. If the alternatives are compared having an ideal pattern or alternative in mind this phenomenon should not occur ([18]). Some scales, methods for calculating the priority vector and synthesis modes have been proposed, in order to minimize the phenomenon. In the specific cases that are reported in this manuscript, we considered that the rank reversal phenomenon is not a serious problem. However, we acknowledge that several authors strongly critic the possibility of occurrence of the rank reversal (e.g., Belton and Gear [19] and Dyer [20]).

Two difficulties with the application of AHP to intervention measures are related to the need of performing a large number of comparisons, when there are many measures, and comparing very different alternatives. In fact, Saaty [7] recommends that comparisons should involve sets of no more than seven elements. In the case of the type of application we are considering, these are important issues, since a large number of alternatives can be identified for each case and it is difficult to compare some alternative measures according to some objectives. Comparing all pairs of proposals according to all the criteria would thus be quite hard.

Some authors have proposed procedures for reducing the number of comparisons. Triantaphyllou [21] suggests a duality procedure for reducing the number of required comparisons. Within this procedure, the typical questions made to the decision maker require her to compare the importance of two criteria in terms of an alternative, instead of comparing two alternatives according to a criterion (as usual in AHP). This procedure reduces the number of required comparisons whenever the number of alternatives is larger than the number of criteria plus one. In the case of our approach, this procedure would reduce the number of required judgments, but the type of comparisons required by the duality procedure was judged to be less intuitive than the usual AHP comparisons, so we did not use this procedure.

Islam and Abdullah [22] propose a procedure for excluding criteria that carry a small weight, and suggest this as a way of reducing the number of required comparisons. In the evaluation of intervention measures, the defined criteria were the result of a preliminary analysis, and were all judged to be important. Apart from that, the exclusion of some criteria would still lead to an unmanageably large number of required comparisons, and would not address the problem of comparing very different alternatives.

A usual way of addressing the problem of having a large number of possibly very different alternatives is through the clustering of alternatives. Saaty [18] describes a method based on the construction of clusters of homogeneous alternatives. After the clusters are built, they are ordered based on the similarity of the alternatives. The alternatives within the first cluster are then compared among themselves, and their priorities are calculated. The alternative belonging to the first cluster that is most similar to the ones belonging to the second one is then placed on the second cluster and the priorities of this "extended" second cluster are determined. Then, an alternative from the second cluster is placed on the third one, and the process goes on until the priorities are calculated for all the clusters. The common element of each two consecutive clusters allows the calculation of priorities that are consistent across the different clusters. With this method we get a set of priorities for all the elements, without having either to compare very large sets of alternatives, or very disparate ones.

The solution for the problem of a large number of alternatives was based on the analysis of the characteristics of the type of application we are considering. The identified intervention measures are usually defined with a specific objective in mind, and are often irrelevant for other objectives. The classical use of AHP considers the comparison of all alternatives on all objectives of the lower level, but in this particular case, it was considered that if an alternative is irrelevant to some criteria, then it can be omitted from the comparisons on those criteria. Apart from significantly reducing the required number of comparisons, this idea also allow us to avoid two other difficulties:

-    It was noticed that the difficulty in comparing alternatives according to an objective arose mostly when the alternatives being compared were irrelevant for the objective. By defining beforehand that irrelevant alternatives would be left out, such difficulties were avoided.

-    When an alternative is irrelevant for an objective, even choosing the lowest values of the comparison scale when making comparisons will allow it to get a positive, albeit small, impact in that objective. In fact, since the alternative is irrelevant for the objective, the correct impact would be null. By leaving the alternative out of the comparisons and defining a null impact, we are avoiding such spurious values for the impact.

In the applications we are considering, alternatives are intervention measures defined with a given objective in mind. So, after defining that some alternatives would be left out of the comparisons concerning some objectives, it was still necessary to define whether an alternative would only be considered for the objective for which it was defined, or for all objectives for which it might be relevant. The latter approach seemed to be the most cautious one, since an alternative might, at least theoretically, have a significant impact in objectives other than the one for which it was defined. In fact, the application cases that were performed showed that:

-    In many cases, each alternative is irrelevant for all objectives but one (the one for which it was designed). This is the case of the first application case presented in the next section.

-    In the cases in which some alternatives are relevant for several objectives, considering only the objective for which the alternatives were defined would often have a very limited impact in the ranking of alternatives. However, in some cases this difference can be substantial. This is the case of the second application case presented in the next section.

It must be noticed that omitting alternatives from the comparisons in some criteria raised a different problem: structural imbalance on the hierarchy. In fact, if the alternatives do not have an impact on all criteria, and if different criteria (subcriteria) have different numbers of subcriteria (alternatives), we are in presence of an unbalanced hierarchy that may somehow bias the results. Such imbalances may be corrected by using the process known as 'structural adjustment': "if not all the subcriteria are used to evaluate every alternative, then the distribution of the value would not be proportionate due to the variation in the number of subcriteria under each criterion" ([7], p. 121). Saaty [7] proposes to adjust the weights of the criteria by multiplying each criterion priority by the relative number of its own subcriteria to the total subcriteria of the level and then to normalize. This simple procedure proposed by Saaty may itself lead to other biases.

We used Saaty's procedure for structural adjustment in some of the analysed cases. The attained results were sometimes considered nonsensical by the consultants and managers and it was harder to justify their use as a basis for the work. Additionally, we stress that the application of AHP to SME diagnostic has a cognitive orientation, that is, what the decision-makers learn in the process is perhaps more important than the rank resulting from the application of AHP. This reduces the impact of the problem of structural imbalance in the results and therefore we chose not to use any adjustment procedure and instead to perform a deep analysis of the results of each application with the managers and consultants.

3   Application Cases of AHP to SME Diagnostic

3.1   Case I – Civil Engineering Company

This application case concerns a company whose activity consists of performing the analysis, verification and validation of construction projects, the management of construction contracting, as well as the inspection or management of constructions sites.

The analysis of the company enabled to identify the current main objective: raising operational results up to a positive level, as their numbers were in the red. The current issues requiring intervention were also identified:
-    difficulties in finding new contracts;
-    due dates of some of the contracts in the current portfolio were expiring;
-    employees felt difficulties in managing their individual time, especially on work overload;
-    communication breakdowns from higher to lower hierarchy (though there were several meetings with clients, the employees were not aware of them neither of the resulting information);
-    there were problems managing documents and archives;
-    several employees reported difficulties in using office applications;
-    there was not enough expertise inside the company to do internal quality audits;
-    there was not enough expertise inside the company for fire security inspection (the company was sub-contracting other companies for this issue).

A tree of objectives was built (presented on Table 2) and the identified intervention measures were the following:
-    IM-1: To reinforce the sales team;
-    IM-2: To improve marketing strategies;
-    IM-3: To improve internal communication between management staff and employees through regular meetings;

-     IM-4: To improve the archives, by introducing a database management system;

-     IM-5: To teach employees about techniques for personal time management and office applications;

-     IM-6: To teach quality control techniques to employees;

-     IM-7: To contract experts on fire security systems and inspections;

-     IM-8: To reduce financing costs by changing short term debt to long term debt.

In this application case, each intervention measure was found to be relevant for just one objective, therefore it was disregarded for the remaining ones. Table 1 presents the results of the application of AHP. Notice that the consistency ratio was acceptable for all comparison matrixes.

Table 1. Tree of objectives and evaluation results for Case I (the values in parenthesis are the global priorities of the measures)

Positive Operational Results (100%)							
Improve Sales Effectiveness (9%)		Improve Productivity (35%)			Reduce Costs (56%)		
		Reduce Unproductive Time (9%)					
IM-1 (8%)	IM-2 (1%)	IM-3 (2%)	IM-4 (7%)	IM-5 (26%)	IM-6 (11%)	IM-7 (34%)	IM-8 (11%)

From Table 1 it is easy to conclude that management must focus on reducing costs by reshaping the debt, contracting experts on fire security, teaching quality control techniques to employees and improve the expertise of employees on personal time management and office applications.

The AHP was primarily used to gain more knowledge about the decision process and not to black-box the choice of intervention measures. Instead of a formal sensitivity analysis, we chose to review the ranking results and the choice of measures with the management and the consultants, in order to make sure these results were sensible. Particularly, in the case of this application, it was analysed whether it was acceptable to choose a set of intervention measures that had no impact in two of the objectives: improvement of sales effectiveness and reduction of unproductive time. It was concluded by management and the consultants that sales effectiveness was not really that relevant, and that the reduction of unproductive time was relevant only for the improvement of productivity, which was taken into account by one of the chosen measures.

Looking at each of the highest ranked measures also led to the conclusion that the results were sensible. Grossman and Helpman [23] state that the decision of whether to integrate or outsource can be seen "... as a trade-off between the transaction costs that stem from search and incomplete contracts on the one hand and the extra governance costs associated with vertical integration on the other." ([23], p. 118). The company was having trouble getting cost-effective external aid with the fire security systems and inspections, and the search and contracting costs were becoming very large, so it made sense to hire employees that might allow the firm to perform these functions without resorting to external help. The company had productivity problems and time management training can indeed have a positive impact on performance (see, e.g., [24], [25]). Quality control training and the reduction of financing costs did also made sense given the importance of reducing costs. So, although the obtained result was not obvious at the outset, the analysis performed after the application of AHP showed that indeed it made sense, taking into account the situation the company was in.

3.2   Case II – Printing Company

This application case concerns a small company whose activity consists of printing documents and other material for institutional communication and marketing. It has three main sections: the accounting section; the pre-printing section, where the materials are prepared to the printing machines; and the production section, where the materials enter the machines to be printed.

After analyzing the current economic and financial state of the company and the business context, a SWOT analysis was performed. This analysis enabled to identify the current issues that needed intervention, in order to increase the revenues.

The identified elements needing intervention were the following:

-      disorganized billing process, in which printed and delivered works were not billed to customers because the accounting section did not know about them;
-      communication breaks between the pre-printing section and the production section;
-      incorrect filling of the production forms;
-      difficulties in finding technical information about previous works;
-      urgent requests disrupted pre-printing section workflow, causing delays;
-      there was a general feeling that the employees where not listened to when problems arose;
-      production employees were under-motivated, as they felt that they were working harder than the employees from the other sections.

A tree of objectives was built, where the main objective of increasing the revenues was identified, as well as two sub-objectives, namely, to improve the billing process and to improve productivity. This latter sub-objective was also divided into other sub-objectives, namely: to improve production effectiveness; to reduce nonproductive times; and to raise employees' satisfaction. This tree is presented in Table 1.

The identified intervention measures were the following:

-      IM-1: To re-design the billing process, possibly by introducing billing software;
-      IM-2: To introduce a better communication channel between production and accounting sections, in order to control deliveries and billing;
-      IM-3: To improve the communication channel between pre-printing and the production sections, in order to avoid breakdowns, thus reducing lead times;
-      IM-4: To emphasize the need for documenting the different works, preferably using digital documenting;
-      IM-5: To improve the archive system, by introducing a database management system;

-     IM-6: To re-design processes in order to avoid urgent requests;
-     IM-7: To improve internal communication;
-     IM-8: To find ways for employees' acknowledgement.

In this application case, it was noticed that some intervention measures contributed for more than one objective. So, two base analyses were performed: one of them considered the impact of each intervention measure only in the objective for which it was defined, and the second considered the impacts of each intervention measure in all objectives for which it might be relevant. Table 2 presents the results of the first analysis and Table 3 presents the results of the second one (the consistency ratio was considered acceptable for all comparison matrixes). For comparison purposes, and since this was not a very large example, it was also decided to perform a classical AHP application in which all the alternative measures were compared according to all criteria. A comparison of the results of all the analyses is presented in Table 4.

Table 2. Tree of objectives and evaluation results for the first analysis of Case II (the values in parenthesis are the global priorities of the measures)

Increase Revenues (100%)							
Improve Billing (67%)		Improve Productivity (33%)					
		Production Effectiveness (20%)		Reducing Unproductive Time (5%)		Employees' Satisfaction (8%)	
IM-1 (50%)	IM-2 (17%)	IM-3 (7%)	IM-4 (13%)	IM-5 (1%)	IM-6 (4%)	IM-7 (4%)	IM-8 (4%)

Table 3. Tree of objectives and evaluation results for the second analysis of Case II (the values in parenthesis are the contribution of each objective to the total impact of the measure)

Increase Revenues (100%)								
Improve Billing (67%)		Improve Productivity (33%)						
		Production Effectiveness (20%)			Reducing Unproductive Time (5%)		Employees' Satisfaction (8%)	
IM-1 (50.0%)	IM-2 (16.7%)	IM-2 (1.6%)	IM-3 (2.1%)	IM-4 (5.0%)	IM-3 (0.5%)	IM-4 (0.9%)	IM-3 (2.9%)	IM-7 (2.9%) IM-8 (2.9%)
		IM-5 (3.3%)	IM-6 (3.6%)	IM-7 (4.0%)	IM-5 (1.1%)	IM-6 (2.8%)		

It is interesting to compare the results of these three analyses. In all cases the highest ranked measure is IM-1 and the second highest is IM-2. However, the impact of these measures (particularly the first one) varies significantly from the first two analyses to the third one. The reason is that the comparison scale ensures that, in the classical AHP application (third analysis), all alternatives will get a positive, albeit small, impact in all objectives. In the most important objective (Improve Billing), the relevant intervention measures, IM-1 and IM-2, will thus have a smaller impact when all measures are compared according to this objective. Additionally, since all other measures are irrelevant to this objective, IM-1 and IM-2 will be considered "extremely more important" than all other measures. But including a set of comparisons that is equal for IM-1 and IM-2 will reduce the difference between their impacts in this objective. Summarizing, the introduction of irrelevant intervention measures IM-3 – IM-8 in the "Improve Billing" objective results in:

-   An increase in the impacts of IM-3 – IM-8 in this objective.
-   A reduction of the sum of the impacts of IM-1 and IM-2.
-   A reduction between the difference of the impacts of IM-1 and IM-2.

Since "Improve Billing" has a very high weight (67%), these effects have a significant influence in the final results, leading to a significant reduction of the impact of IM-1, an increase of IM-2, and also an increase in the impacts of most of the other measures. In fact, when analyzing these results, it was considered that IM-1 had an unreasonably low impact in analysis 3.

Table 4. Comparison of results for the three analysis of Case II (First analysis: each intervention measure assigned to the objective for which it was defined; Second analysis: each intervention measure assigned to the objectives for which it contributes; Third analysis: each intervention measure assigned to all objectives)

Intervention Measure	First Analysis		Second Analysis		Third Analysis	
	Impact	Rank	Impact	Rank	Impact	Rank
IM-1	50%	1st	50%	1st	31%	1st
IM-2	17%	2nd	18%	2nd	23%	2nd
IM-3	7%	4th	5%	6th	9%	4th
IM-4	13%	3rd	6%	5th	10%	3rd
IM-5	1%	8th	4%	7th	5%	8th
IM-6	4%	5th	7%	3rd	6%	7th
IM-7	4%	5th	7%	3rd	7%	5th
IM-8	4%	5th	3%	8th	7%	5th

Comparing now the results of analyses 1 and 2, it is noticeable that, while the two highest ranked measures have similar impacts in both analyses, there are important differences in the impacts of the remaining measures. For example, IM-4, which was ranked in third place in analysis 1, drops to fifth place in analysis 2, with less than half the impact it had in analysis 1. The reason for this comes from the impacts of the different measures in the second most important objective, "Production Effectiveness". Only IM-3 and IM-4 were defined with this objective in mind, so only these measures were considered for this objective in the first analysis. However, although measures IM-6 and IM-7 were defined with other objectives in mind, they may also have a very significant impact in this objective. So, when IM-6 and IM-7 are considered for the "Production Effectiveness" objective, the impacts of IM-3 and IM-4 in this objective will decrease and IM-6 and IM-7 achieve a significant impact in this objective. Given the weight of this objective, this leads to a significant increase of the weights of IM-6 and IM-7 and a decrease of the weights of IM-3 and IM-4.

So, the question regarding analyses 1 and 2 was: if you can choose either IM-3 and IM-4 (as suggested by the first analysis) or IM-6 and IM-7 (as suggested by the second one), which pair of measures should you choose? A careful analysis led to the conclusion that IM-6 and IM-7 would be a better choice, since these measures would have a very significant impact in the "Production Effectiveness" and also some impact in the less important objectives "Reducing Unproductive Time" and "Employees' Satisfaction".

So, from the analysis of the results it was concluded by the management and the consultants that management should focus on improving the billing system, both re-designing the billing process and improving the coordination between the production and accounting sections. In fact, it was acknowledged that the billing activity was the main weakness of the company and, given the importance of proper business processes in the company activities (see, e.g., [26], p.4), the most urgent measures were related to the improvement of processes that related to this activity (both the billing process and communication processes related to this activity). Avoiding urgent requests and improving internal communications were also considered relevant intervention measures that should be followed in order to achieve an increase in revenues.

4   Conclusions

In this paper we discussed the application of AHP to intervention measures in Portuguese SMEs and we presented the results of the application of AHP to two Portuguese SMEs. These intervention measures result from external diagnostics performed under the QREN program. The AHP application enabled to acquire more knowledge about the decision process, to rank the intervention measures and to focus on the more promising ones.

An important problem faced in this application of AHP was the large number of required comparisons. The fact that intervention measures are usually defined with a given objective in mind, and are often irrelevant for other objectives, led us to define that intervention measures should be excluded from comparisons in criteria for which they are irrelevant (defining a null impact for the intervention measure in such criteria). This also reduced the difficulties in comparing alternatives and avoided some biases resulting from the maximum and minimum values of the comparison scale being used.

The comparison between the classical application of AHP (comparing all alternatives according to all lower level objectives) and excluding alternatives from criteria for which they are irrelevant showed that the latter procedure tends to more reasonable results, as expected.

When analysing whether an alternative should only be considered for the objective for which it was defined, or for all objectives for which it might be relevant, we concluded that it would be better to follow the latter approach. Although in many cases the results of both approaches were quite similar, in some other cases there were important differences. We showed an application case (Case II) in which the latter approach does indeed produce more sensible results.

The AHP was applied to several other Portuguese SMEs, of different sectors of activity, but the results were not presented in this paper. We stress that, since the approach we followed is based on an analysis of management issues, instead of specific sector-dependent issues, the type of adjustments that may be required when applying it to different companies is quite limited – we were able to apply the same general framework to all the companies we considered.

It must be emphasized that some of these Portuguese SMEs also operate abroad (Europe, Brazil and Portuguese speaking Africa) and so for some of them the economic environment is not only the Portuguese economy. However, we did not study the differences (cultural, management education, etc.) from Portuguese SMEs to non-Portuguese SMEs. Probably some adjustments to the proposed general methodology must be introduced in order to adapt it to other cultures. Namely, the meetings among managers, consultants and employees were rather informal and the discussions were conducted in an unstructured way: this type of behavior is typical of Portuguese SMEs.

The presented cases are deemed enough to understand the advantages of the AHP use and also to start the assessment of which are recurring cases. This observation enabled us to start the design of an information system for helping on SMEs diagnostic process. By documenting several cases, it is possible to select groups and sub-groups of intervention measures along with groups and sub-groups of issues that require intervention.

As future research, the general idea is to build an interactive web application where managers can have access to SMEs cases and be able to extract related information. In this way, managers (without the help of hired consultants) can choose the intervention measures that better fit their particular case.

Finally, it is important to stress that this methodology, or any web application we may define, cannot completely replace the role of a human decision-maker. By using a flexible method that was designed to be applied without prior knowledge of the number of measures to be implemented, or the available budget, and that depends on comparisons made by a decision-maker, there is sometimes the risk of reaching unreasonable results. For example, the results may lead to situations in which an important objective is not addressed by any of the chosen intervention measures. So, in some cases, it may make sense not to choose the intervention measures exactly using their global ranking, but make some adjustments to that ranking (e.g., if an important objective is not addressed by any measure, considering replacing the lowest ranked chosen measure by the measure that contributes most to the objective).

Acknowledgments. This work has been partially supported by FCT under project grant PEst-C/EEI/UI0308/2011. Rita Encarnação from CH Business Consulting, SA, facilitated the work on the presented cases. Francisco Antunes helped on the use of the English language in earlier versions of the manuscript.

References

1. Associação Empresarial de Portugal: Manual de Organização e Funcionamento - Programa Formação PME 2011-2012. Câmara de Comércio e Indústria (2011)
2. Associação Empresarial de Águeda: AEA- Formação de Empresários (2010), http://www.aea.com.pt/formempresarios.html (accessed in January 2012)
3. Saaty, T.L.: The Analytic Hierarchy Process. McGraw Hill, New York (1980)
4. Moreno-Jiménez, J.M., Aguarón, J., Escobar, M.T., Turon, A.: Multicriteria Procedural Rationality on SISDEMA. Eur. J. Oper. Res. 119(2), 388–403 (1999)

5. Moreno-Jiménez, J.M., Aguarón, J., Escobar, M.T.: Metodología Científica en Valoración y Selección Ambiental. Pesq. Oper. 21(1), 1–16 (2001)
6. Dong, Y., Xu, Y., Li, H., Dai, H.: A Comparative Study of the Numerical Scales and the Prioritization Methods in AHP. Eur. J. Oper. Res. 186(1), 229–242 (2008)
7. Saaty, T.L.: Fundamentals of Decision Making and Priority Theory with the Analytic Hierarchy Process. RWS Publications, Pittsburgh (1994)
8. Godinho, P., Costa, J.P., Fialho, J., Afonso, R.: Some Issues about the Application of the Analytic Hierarchy Process to R&D Project Selection, Global Bus. Econ. Rev. 13(1), 26–41 (2011)
9. Bana Costa, C., Vansnick, J.: MACBETH - An Interactive Path Towards the Construction of Cardinal Value Functions. Int. T. Oper. Res. 1(4), 489–500 (1994)
10. Barzilai, J.: Measurement and Preference Function Modelling. Int. T. Oper. Res. 12(2), 173–183 (2005)
11. Harker, P., Vargas, L.: The Theory of Ratio Scale Estimation: Saaty's Analytic Hierarchy Process. Manage. Sci. 33(11), 1383–1403 (1987)
12. Lootsma, F.A.: Conflict Resolution via Pairwise Comparison of Concessions. Eur. J. Oper. Res. 40(1), 109–116 (1989)
13. Salo, A., Hämäläinen, R.: On the Measurement of Preferences in the Analytic Hierarchy Process. J. Multi-Criteria Decis. Anal. 6(6), 309–319 (1997)
14. Ma, D., Zheng, X.: 9/9–9/1 Scale Method of AHP. In: Proceedings of the 2nd International Symposium on the AHP, vol. 1, pp. 197–202. University of Pittsburgh, Pittsburgh (1991)
15. Beynon, M.: An Analysis of Distributions of Priority Values from Alternative Comparison Scales within AHP. Eur. J. Oper. Res. 140(1), 104–117 (2002)
16. Ishizaka, A., Labib, A.: Review of the Main Developments in the Analytic Hierarchy Process. Expert Syst. Appl. 38(11), 14336–14345 (2011)
17. Millet, I., Saaty, T.L.: On the Relativity of Relative Measures – Accommodating both Rank Preservation and Rank Reversals in the AHP. Eur. J. Oper. Res. 121(1), 205–212 (2000)
18. Saaty, T.L.: That is not the Analytic Hierarchy Process: What the AHP is and what it is not. J. Multi-Criteria Decis. Anal. 6(6), 324–335 (1997)
19. Belton, V., Gear, T.: On a Shortcoming of Saaty's Method of Analytic Hierarchies. Omega-Int. J. Manage. S. 11(3), 228–230 (1983)
20. Dyer, J.: A Clarification of 'Remarks on the Analytic Hierarchy Process. Manage. Sci. 36(3), 274–275 (1990)
21. Triantaphyllou, E.: Reduction of Pairwise Comparisons in Decision Making via Duality Approach. J. Multi-Criteria Decis. Anal. 8(6), 299–310 (1999)
22. Islam, R., Abdullah, N.: Management Decision-Making by the Analytic Hierarchy Process: A Proposed Modification for Large-Scale Problems. J. Int. Bus. Enterpren. Dev. 3(1/2), 18–40 (2006)
23. Grossman, G.M., Helpman, E.: Integration versus Outsourcing in Industry Equilibrium. Q. J. Econ. 117(1), 85–120 (2002)
24. Orpen, C.: The Effect of Time-Management Training on Employee Attitudes and Behavior: A Field Experiment. J. Psychol. 128(4), 393–396 (1994)
25. Green, P., Skinner, D.: Does Time Management Training Work? An Evaluation. International Journal of Training and Development 9(2), 124–139 (2005)
26. Weske, M.: Business Process Management, 2nd edn. Springer (2012)

A DSS Solution for Integrated Automated Bidding, Subcontractor Selection and Project Scheduling

Alireza Pakgohar, Stephen J. Childe, and David Z. Zhang

College of Engineering, Mathematics and Physical Sciences
University of Exeter, Exeter, UK
{A.Pakgohar,S.J.Childe,D.Z.Zhang}@exeter.ac.uk

Abstract. Subcontractor Selection and Project Planning are two essential decision stages in the construction industry. Bidding leads to the selection of subcontractors. At the next stage, project planners communicate and coordinate with selected subcontractors to plan the project. These processes generally provide the initial overall project plan and schedule for a building project, and conventional methods lack flexibility and integration. In this study, we propose a new decision making framework and present an integrated decision support system (DSS) to facilitate concurrent decision making in these interrelated processes. An assessment of the system by project managers at the case study company indicates that the system is capable of greatly improving the bidding, subcontractor selection and project planning processes in a holistic (integrated) framework. The system can be applied generally in the construction industry.

Keywords: Construction Industry, Bid Processing, Subcontractor Selection, Multi-objective Optimisation, GA, Pareto front.

1   Introduction

Nowadays, intuitive interactive decision support systems are everywhere and in every context. One reason for their popularity is that rather than make a decision and give the optimal solution to the user, they help managers to make an optimal or near optimal decision for complex systems by providing a user interface to allow the user to interact with the system at each stage of the process and determine a preferred solution.

Project management is one area where software packages have been increasingly developed and used both as desktop software and web-based systems in recent years[1],[2]. One of the essential areas in project management, particularly in the construction industry is the bidding process. Portfolio managers who deal directly with clients need reliable and quick information to estimate the price of the bid and put forward their bid to the clients very quickly. Most of the effort in the tendering process is focused solely on estimating the cost. Therefore, when they have been appointed to the project, contractors usually seek a solution to finish the project by the due date given by the client. With respect to bid pricing and estimation, the construction company generally breaks down the job and sends the request for inquiry

J.E. Hernández et al. (Eds.): EWG-DSS 2012, LNBIP 164, pp. 72–85, 2013.

to its prequalified subcontractors. Traditionally, it has been usual to select the minimum price bid. However, recently several methods have been developed to include other managerial aspects for subcontractor selection [3] [4]. Some software packages based on DSS facilitate subcontractor ranking and scoring. These systems help project managers to rank the subcontractors based on their performance evaluated by cost, time and quality [3].

In current practice, when a contractor has been awarded the contract, the project planners are assigned to the project and a project schedule is developed through collaboration and communication between the project management team and the subcontractors. The processes of bidding, subcontractor selection and project planning/scheduling have been undertaken in a sequential manner that takes a long time. In addition, at the time of tendering the portfolio manager usually has no reliable estimate of the project makespan and works with the deadlines that are set by the client, regardless of the collaboration with subcontractor about time estimation.

In the current study, we present a new DSS that integrated these processes in a single framework that helps to achieve better estimation of the cost and time of the project along with selecting the appropriate subcontractors to accomplish the project. The project planning and subcontractor selection are undertaken concurrently and the automated bidding process that helps project managers to send and receive work packages to and from subcontractors facilitate these processes in a holistic approach.

While Fig. 1 depicts the proposed integrated framework the other sections are explaining each of these interrelated processes.

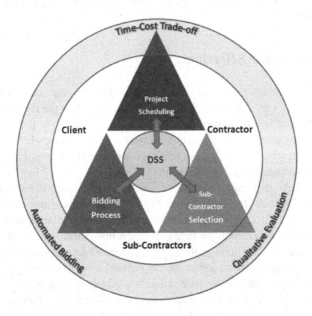

Fig. 1. Integrated DSS Framework

2   The Bidding Process in the Construction Industry

The bidding process is a critical task in the construction industry. The process is initiated by client's request. The main or general contractors (GCs) must respond to the request in a limited time accurately and precisely. Estimating the bidding price in a competitive market environment while managing other projects is a complex challenge confronting the portfolio managers at the GCs.

To make an accurate estimation, the portfolio managers must break down the project into work packages and identify the specialised subcontractors (SCs) or traders with skills and resources to undertake each package. They usually follow a similar approach to the client, i.e. sending the request for inquiry to the subcontractors and suppliers, communicating with them, selecting the best bid for each work package, summing up the prices from each work package to come up with total price, and finally adding required costs such as indirect and managerial costs, tax, contingency costs and profit margin. They can then submit the bid to the client. Arslan et al. [3] describe this process in seven phases. Although they did not present e-bidding, their phases demonstrated all of the steps that should be implemented to achieve a successful contract. In this process, subcontractor selection is based on the low bid price approach that for many years has been widely used in many countries. Furthermore, in this process, no attention is given to the time estimation and duration for the work package as offered by the subcontractor. For selecting subcontractors, as long as the due date is met only one dimension, cost, is being considered. In the next section, we review some aspects of the subcontractor's bid selection and present our improved method.

3   Subcontractor Selection

As each main contractor's bid to the client relies on the collected bids from subcontractors, it is very important for the contractor to select the right subcontractors. The low-bid method is a traditional and widely-used approach. In the low-bid method "the contract is awarded to the firm submitting the lowest responsible bid"[4]. In the competitive construction market, subcontractors try offer the lowest possible estimates for their work packages to win the projects[4].

In the case where there are a number of bids received from different subcontractors, there might be some bids that are out of range. Particularly, GCs may receive some bids that seem to be unrealistic. The reasons why a subcontractor submits such out of range bids could be either accidentally or deliberately. In this situation, choosing the low-bid strategy brings risks and difficulties for all of the stakeholders because the subcontractor may not be able to perform the job at the pre-defined cost, time and quality. Therefore some scholars and practitioners propose different methods to help with bid selection [4]. The average bidding method is a good alternative to overcome this drawback. Those who adhere to this method believe that a price close to the average should offer a fair price to the owner and allow the contractor to perform the work at specified quality and at a reasonable profit. It should be noted that each country has a particular approach that is suit for that country. For instance, in Peru, they use the general concept of the average bid pricing in this way: "if less than three bids are received, a bidding agency may award the contract to the lowest bidder. When three or more bids are received, the average of all bids and the base budget are calculated, and bids that lie 10% above and below this average are eliminated. A second average of the remaining bids and the base budget is calculated, and the bid closest to but below the second average is the winner" [4]. A new method namely "Below Average Bidding" has been presented [4]. This method provides more information choices for selecting one bid among different received bids.

Apart from these commonly used approaches there is another stream of subcontractor selection that focuses on qualitative aspects. Particularly, some scholars propose methods that consider risk and using qualitative approaches to evaluate subcontractors and calculate a score for each subcontractor in each expertise area [3],[2]. Although their approaches consider more parameters to facilitate subcontractor evaluation, the time and cost of each bid are evaluated on a qualitative Likert scale.

In this study we propose a method for subcontractor selection considering both qualitative and quantitative measurements. This method consists of four steps:

i) Scoring the subcontractors by a qualitative approach,

ii) Receiving the bids from the selected subcontractors who pass the minimum required qualitative score,

iii) Evaluating the bids content and rejecting outliers,

iv) Conducting a time-cost optimization to select the best combination of the subcontractors using a Time/Cost trade-off shown in a Pareto-front curve.

First, a qualitative evaluation is conducted to allocate scores. We adapted WEBSES [3] to evaluate each subcontractor on a Likert scale for time, cost, quality and adequacy calculated from their previous contract rather than taking to account their current bid. The main idea is that evaluating the quality and adequacy along with cost and time before performing a project is more subjective and it may be biased according to the evaluator's attitudes. However after finishing a project, the evaluator could make a better judgement based on the real performance of the subcontractor. Therefore this qualitative analysis could be applied for subcontractor selection process in the next project. After pre-evaluation of the subcontractors by the WEBSES method, the final rank will be shown. This is facilitated by our prototype software. The project manager is then able to select those subcontractors with a better score and send the Request for Bid (RFB) to them. The RFB is sent electronically to the subcontractors and they have chance to compete. Their submitted bids are collected electronically through the e-mail system "Microsoft Outlook" and directly update the database of bids.

Following the case study interview, it became clear that the users would be greatly helped if the system would assist the user by recognising the outlier bids which the user may consider deleting. This is the second step of the selection process. Those bids that are lower or higher by a certain percentage defined by the project manager (e.g. 20%) of the average price of current bids or of historical bids in the database will be identified at this stage. Therefore, at the end of this process, the GC has a number of bids to proceed to the next stage rather than only one bid and its subcontractor. This approach allows both parts of each bid, cost and time, to be properly assessed, rather than focussing on solely cost and neglecting "time" as described in [4]. In addition, although in qualitative approaches [3], time and cost are both considered together, there is no way to make a trade off between them across the set of received bids for all of the work packages.

In the next step, a time-cost trade-off combinatorial problem is presented that is adapted for the bidding process. This model can be solved to find the Pareto-front curve which shows the optimal solutions and helps project managers, project portfolio managers and clients to compare them according to makespan and total cost of the project. This adds alternatives to the negotiations for the GC company because they have visibility of the range of time and cost options that help clients to make their final decision. The final decision of the client and management team in selecting a solution has the effect of specifying both the general framework of the project plan and, at the same time, selecting the subcontractors. The general concept is depicted in Fig. 2.

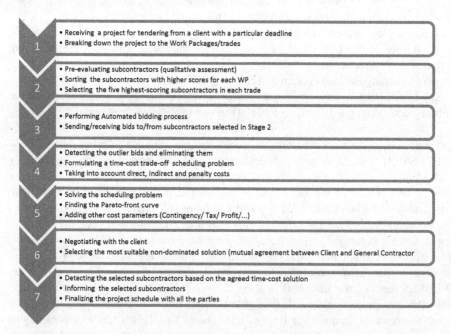

Fig. 2. The integrated bidding process, subcontractor selection and project scheduling model

In contrast with the current practices in construction industry, where subcontractor selection is conducted by taking into account only cost elements of the bids [4], or only qualitative factors such as [3], this method is exploiting qualitative scores of the subcontractors first and then optimising the combination of selected subcontractors to minimise time and cost of the project simultaneously. Three important factors; the subcontractor's score and the cost and time elements of each bid are considered in our model.

In the next section, we will show how a time-cost trade off problem can be utilised to achieve this goal. To do this, we adapt the generalised discrete time-cost problem (GDTCTP) [5], [6] to suit the model for real construction bidding situation and provide use of NSGA2 [7] to find the Pareto-front solution.

4   Project Scheduling Time-Cost Trade-Off with Generalized Precedence Constrained

In the context of project planning and scheduling, the minimal time to complete a project can be calculated based upon its critical activities. In the time-cost trade-off problem, the time duration of each activity can vary as a function of cost. For example, the duration of time can be shortened by deploying more labour and trucks to groundwork in a construction project. It is clear that, this in turn needs more financial expenditure. In the bidding process, where each work package should be allocated to only one subcontractor, each rival subcontractor may offer a different estimate of the cost depending on the amount of the resources that they aimed to use. This gives rise to different time estimation as well. Therefore selecting the subcontractors is a process that needs to be considered as a time-cost trade off problem where the combination of the selected subcontractors for all of the work packages could affect not only the total cost of the project but also the total project's makespan. Since each subcontractor's bid entails both cost and time, we propose to make a decision to select all of the sub-contractors for all of the work packages of the project together, in view of the combined cost and the combined project schedule, rather than selecting them individually which could lead to a sub-optimal overall solution.

In the execution of projects, work packages (WPs) are subject to generalised precedence relation constraints with time lead/lag existing between WP predecessor and successor. The time lag between two WPs (i) and (j) is the time frame that WP (j) can start or finish when its immediate predecessor has already started or finished [8].

To determine the existence of a time-feasible schedule, the earliest start schedule (ESS) for each activity needs to be calculated. This is obtained by determine the longest path from the dummy start (node 1) to that activity's node. This is not the case in multi-mode where each mode leads to different activity duration. The longest path between activities will depend on the mode of execution of each activity.

In this work, we adapt the mathematical formulation of GDTCTP [6] and proposed multi-objective functions, as follows:

A linear-integer programming LP/IP formulation with existence of two objective functions is employed to explore the Pareto-Front curve. A zero-one variable x_{im} is defined for each work package (WP) to represent allocating only one winner to the job. The first objective function of the model represents the project cost and is formulated as follows:

The project start at date 0 and the deadline defined by the client be DD.

Let TC = total cost for each single project, then from the parameters given, a mixed integer programming model for one project is given by:

Minimise: $TC = \sum_{i=1}^{N} \sum_{m=1}^{B(i)} c_{im} * x_{im} + IC * f_N + P * T$ (1)

Minimise: f_N (2)

Where i= WP index in a project; N= is total number of WPs in a project; m = bid indicator; B(i) = total number of all received bids for WP(i); c_{im} = cost of executing WP(i) based on bid m ; x_{im} = 1 if bid m is selected for WP(i) or 0 otherwise; IC = indirect cost of the project per day; P = penalty cost per day; I = incentive bonus; f_N= finishing time of the project; DD = client deadline of the project; $T = \max(0, f_N - DD)$, tardiness of the project.

Eq. 1 represents the minimisation of the total cost of a project while Eq. 2 indicates the minimisation of the total time as the second objective function.

The constraints of the model are presented by the following equations:

$$\sum_{m=1}^{B(i)} x_{im} = 1, \qquad \forall i \in N \tag{3}$$

$$f_i - s_i = \sum_{m=1}^{B(i)} d_{im} * x_{im} \geq 0, \qquad \forall i \in N \tag{4}$$

$$s_i + SS_{ij} \leq s_j, \qquad \forall (i,j) \in E_{SS} \tag{5}$$

$$s_i + SF_{ij} \leq f_j, \qquad \forall (i,j) \in E_{SF} \tag{6}$$

$$f_i + FS_{ij} \leq s_j, \qquad \forall (i,j) \in E_{FS} \tag{7}$$

$$f_i + FF_{ij} \leq f_j, \qquad \forall (i,j) \in E_{FF} \tag{8}$$

$$f_N \geq f_i, \qquad \forall i \in N \tag{9}$$

$$s_i \geq 0, \qquad \forall i \in N \tag{10}$$

$$s_0 = 0 \tag{11}$$

where f_i =finish time of WP (i), s_i =start time of WP (i), d_{im} = duration of WP (i) based on bid m, j = successor WP to WP(i) in a project ; SS_{ij} = time lead/lag between start of WP(i) and start of WP(j), E_{SS} =set of SS precedence relation, SF_{ij} = time lead/lag between start of WP (i) and finish of WP(j); E_{SF} =set of SF precedence relation, FS_{ij} = time lead/lag between finish of WP(i) and start of WP(j); E_{FS} = set of FS precedence relation , FF_{ij} = time lead/lag between finish of WP(i) and finish of WP(j); E_{FF} = set of FF precedence relation.

Eq. 3 ensures that each WP will be assigned to only one subcontractor among all received bids. Eq.4 relates start and finishing time of each WP (i) to the selected bid. Eqs. 5-8 indicate the time lag/lead between activities in the project. Eqs. 9-11 set the start and finish time of the each WP(i).

4.1   Overview of Solution Algorithms

The time cost trade-off problem (TCTP) has been addressed for many years. While some scholars provided mathematical programming models such as dynamic programming, linear programming and integer programming LP/IP hybrid, there is an argument that these methods cannot efficiently obtain optimal solutions for large-scale networks [9]. In addition they may easily get trapped into local optima [10]. Because of these drawbacks of exact solution approaches, many scholars use heuristic and metaheuristic algorithms such as tabu search approach and genetic algorithm (GA). A comprehensive survey of different approaches to single objective TCTP is presented in [11].

There is also a large amount of work using bio-inspired approaches in which minimization of both cost and time as two objective functions are considered. These include Ant Colony optimization (ANC) [12], the Particle Swarm Optimization (PSO) [13] and Harmony Search (HS) optimization [14] methods. These have been applied to gain the optimal Pareto-set solution. The multi objective genetic algorithm is one of the most applied methods in the literature [9],[10],[15]. However, only a few studies in the field of time cost trade off problem take into account the generalized precedence relationship (GPTCTP) between activities [6], [16], [17]. Therefore, we utilize a well known multi objective genetic algorithm namely NSGA2 to achieve Pareto-front solution for the problem GPTCTP that we have proposed for subcontractor selection and project scheduling. The following section describes the concept of NSGA2 and explains how we utilize it to tackle to our problem.

4.2   Non-dominated Sorting Genetic Algorithm (NSGA2)

NSGA2 is a generalization of the genetic algorithm (GA) for multi objective optimization (MOO). Similar to the single objective GA (SOGA), it is based on a simulation of the natural selection and population genetics that needs three main functions for each generation namely selection, combination and mutation where each chromosome represents a certain solution [18]. In contrast with SOGA, there is a set of non-dominated solutions in MOO, where none of the members of that set could dominate the others. A particular solution is said to 'dominate' the other solution in the population if it is at least as good as the latter in every dimension and better in at least one dimension (objective). NSGA2 is a fast approach for ranking the non-dominated solutions [7]. It also calculates a measure namely 'crowding distance' for each solution [7]. At the selection stage, both rank and crowding distance are used to generate a new population. In each iteration, fitness functions are calculated to provide relevant information for the ranking stage. The iterations are terminated if a predetermined number of generations are computed. In this work we use the NSGA2 to develop a Pareto-front curve that shows the best compromising solutions between cost and time. In our construction planning problem, each WP is allocated to one subcontractor/trader, and as in [9] we define the chromosome in such a way that it represents the possibility of allocating different eligible subcontractors to each WP. In the next section we explain the implementation of the proposed integrated DSS.

5   Proposed DSS

In this section, we demonstrate the proposed software by providing some snapshots of the dialog boxes. The software was designed in the Microsoft Access 2007 environment and captured the benefits of integration with other Microsoft Office packages including Excel and Outlook.

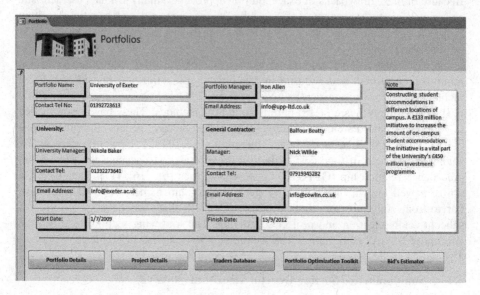

Fig. 3. Defining portfolios

The proposed model and its corresponding DSS software were developed gradually by conducting a case study in UPP Ltd, a market leader construction company that specialises in construction of student accommodation. The company has currently over £1 billion-worth of contracts across the UK's universities to establish around 35000 student accommodation rooms by 2020. Through thorough interviews with project manager and construction subcontractors as well as massive observation that made from undergoing projects the idea was gradually developed and verified by the practitioners.

In the software, portfolios can be defined along with their corresponding projects. In Fig. 3 we show the general specifications of the portfolio in operation at the time of the study at the University of Exeter. The project lasted for 3 years, "The £133 million initiative represented one of the largest property transactions finalised during 2009, involving more than £112 million of funding" [19]. It was one part of the largest development programmes that the University of Exeter has planned. "The initiative is a vital part of the University's £450 million investment programme" [20].

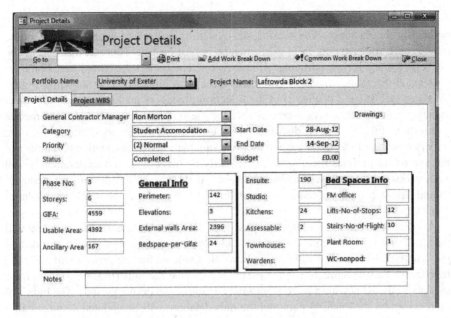

Fig. 4. Defining projects and their work packages

Fig. 4 presents one of the projects making up the university portfolio, a 6-storey block of 4550 square metres including 190 en-suite student rooms located at Lafrowda, the west corner of the University of Exeter campus. The work breakdown of the project based on the required traders is accessed through a tab from this screen.

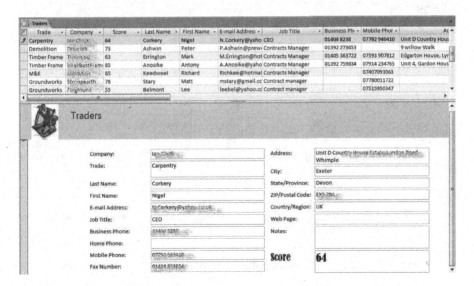

Fig. 5. Defining trades and scoring them

Fig. 5 demonstrates how the traders, subcontractors and manufacturers can be defined in the database. The scoring sub-system is utilized to assign an appropriate rank to each trader based on its performance in past project. This is a measure of the GC's preference for the particular subcontractor. The traders are sorted based on their scores and the project manager can select those with higher rank as shown in Fig. 6. This step (see stage 2 of Fig. 2) of the selection process is qualitative and the project manager's behaviour plays a crucial role for the rest of the process. An interactive dialog box (Fig. 6) will be displayed for the project manager to select/deselect the traders based on their rank, the number of available traders, the market situation and the number of projects that the GC is currently involved with. These parameters will be addressed in our future studies, however in the meantime, the project manager should apply his/her judgement, knowledge and experience for selecting potential subcontractors.

According to Stage 3 of the proposed model (Fig. 2), the tender package will be transferred electronically to the SCs selected in the first step. The software and the database were easily linked to Microsoft Outlook for the purpose of the data transfer to the subcontractors, i.e. to send and receive the bids (Fig. 6). Traders have to reply to the RFB within a pre-determined deadline (tendering period). The bids will be received by the email system and the bids database will be updated automatically. The next step of the interactive DSS solution is assessing to find the outlier bids. Further to this stage, a time-cost trade-off scheduling problem will be formulated and solved (Stage 5, Fig. 2). The automated link between Access and Excel allowed us to utilize SolveXL [21] as an optimization unit in the DSS for covering the fifth stage of Fig. 2.

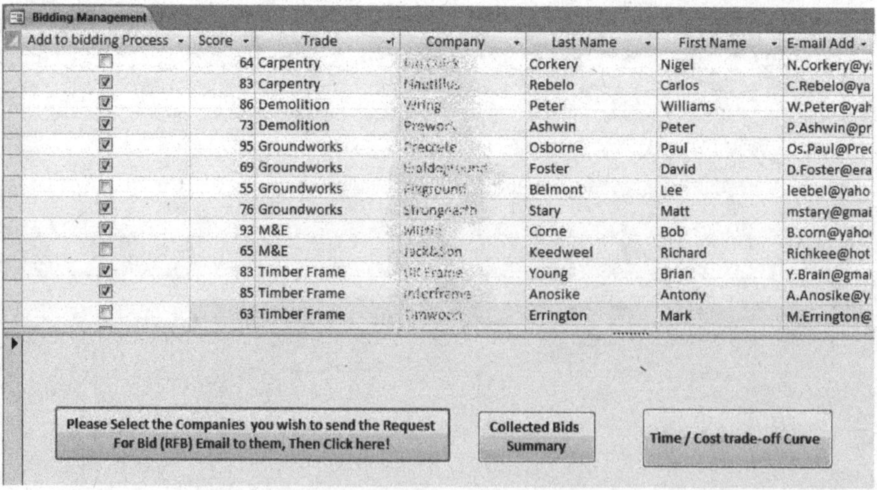

Fig. 6. Selecting the SCs based in their score and sending RFB electronically

Due to the requirements of confidentiality in the building project which prevent showing the actual data, we present in Fig. 7. an illustration of the Pareto-front curve using test data, as provided by SolveXL. Each point on the chart represents an alternative project solution, ranging from more expensive, shorter durations at the top left to longer duration cheaper solutions at bottom right. The user can click on any particular solution in the curve to come up with project schedule and its corresponding subcontractors.

The software and the results were presented to the University's contract manager and the UPP-Ltd's Construction Director and Project Managers. The four experienced managers were able to verify the proposed model and its corresponding DSS solution. They found that the ability to select project options and have the complete schedule produced was a significant step forward from their current practice. In particular they commented on the advantage of being able to know the cost implications and possibilities for accelerating a project.

The contributions of the work are also in line with the gap found in the literature where bidding process, subcontractor selection and project scheduling, three different but interconnected area of research, are addressed separately. The authors were unable to find any research, framework or toolkit to demonstrate the integration of these processes. With this holistic approach we provide the main advantages of the proposed framework and the DSS software as facilitating the bidding process by coordinating with different subcontractors, facilitating the subcontractor selection by controlling the bids quality while optimising more promised time-cost options to offer to the clients.

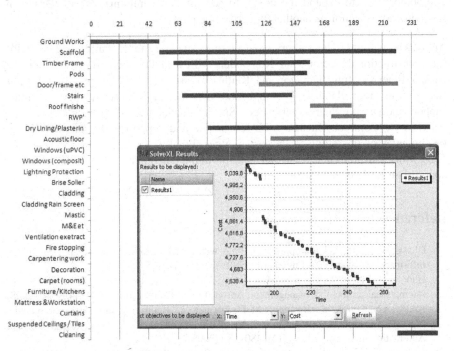

Fig. 7. Selecting one of the solutions from the Pareto-front Curve and its corresponding Gantt Chart

Finally, the other main benefit of the proposed model is that the approach generates the master schedule that determines the time window for total project, which should be set between client and general contractor, as well as coordinating the work packages that are conducted by different specialised traders/subcontractors.

6   Conclusion and Further Research

In this paper an automated bidding process along with a framework for subcontractor selection and project planning in the tendering stage was proposed. These sequential stages could be coordinated by project portfolio, project manager, and quantity surveyor and project planner. This framework enables construction project management to be more agile in response to the potential clients in such a way that the portfolio manager can offer an accurate bid to the clients while at the same time the project manager selects appropriate subcontractors to deal with different work packages. The framework has been introduced and the result was verified by one of the market leading companies specialized in the construction of student accommodation.

For future work, the authors plan to implement the DSS software in other industries to verify its applicability in a wider range. In addition time-cost-risk trade-off could be the other research line which could improve the subcontractor selection. The authors aim to expand the model to accommodate minimization of the risk in subcontractor selection as another objective function.

Acknowledgement. The authors would like to sincerely thank Paul Goddard (UPP-Ltd Construction Director) and Ron Allen (UPP-Ltd Portfolio Manager) and also Nick Wilkie, Portfolio Director and Keith Gazzard, Project Manager from Balfour Beatty who are collaborating with us through the case study by their continued support and sharing their experiences. Special thanks are due to Nicola Baker, the University's Contract Manager who has helped and supported the author from the first minutes of this study to the last minutes. Finally, we thank Dragan Savić and Mark Morley from Centre for Water Systems at the University of Exeter for providing appropriate guidelines for using SolveXL.

References

1. Chassiakos, A.P., Sakellaropoulos, S.P.: A web-based system for managing construction information. Advances in Engineering Software 39(11), 865–876 (2008)
2. Han, S.H., Kim, D.Y., Kim, H., Jang, W.S.: A web-based integrated system for international project risk management. Automation in Construction 17(3), 342–356 (2008)
3. Arslan, G., Kivrak, S., Birgonul, M.T., Dikmen, I.: Improving sub-contractor selection process in construction projects: Web-based sub-contractor evaluation system (WEBSES). Automation in Construction 17(4), 480–488 (2008)
4. Ioannou, P., Awwad, R.: Below-Average Bidding Method. Journal of Construction Engineering and Management 139(9), 936–947 (2010)

5. De Reyck, B., Herroelen, W.: The multi-mode resource-constrained project scheduling problem with generalized precedence relations. European Journal of Operational Research (119), 538–556 (1999)
6. Chassiakos, A., Sakellaropoulos, S.: Time-cost optimization of construction projects with generalized activity constraints. Journal of Construction Engineering and Management 131(10), 1115–1124 (2005)
7. Deb, K., Pratap, A., Agarwal, S., Meyarivan, T.: A Fast and Elitist Multiobjective Genetic Algorithm: NSGA 2. IEEE Transactions on Evolutionary Computation 6(2), 182–197 (2002)
8. Elmaghraby, S., Kamburowski, J.: The analysis of activity networks under generalized precedence relations (GPRs). Management Science 38(9), 1245–1263 (1992)
9. Feng, C., Liu, L., Burns, S.: Using genetic algorithms to solve construction time-cost trade-off problems. Journal of Computing in Civil Engineering 11(3), 184–189 (1997)
10. Zheng, D.: Applying a genetic algorithm-based multiobjective approach for time-cost optimization. Journal of Construction Engineering and Management 130(2), 168–176 (2004)
11. Węglarz, J., Józefowska, J., Mika, M., Waligóra, G.: Project scheduling with finite or infinite number of activity processing modes – A survey. European Journal of Operational Research 208(3), 177–205 (2011)
12. Xiong, Y., Kuang, Y.: Applying an ant colony optimization algorithm-based multiobjective approach for time-cost trade-off. Journal of Construction Engineering and Management 134(2), 153–156 (2008)
13. Yang, I.T.: Using elitist particle swarm optimization to facilitate bicriterion time-cost trade-off analysis. Journal of Construction Engineering and Management 133(7), 498–505 (2007)
14. Geem, Z.: Multiobjective optimization of time-cost trade-off using harmony search. Journal of Construction Engineering and Management 136(6), 711–717 (2009)
15. Ghoddousi, P., Eshtehardian, E., Jooybanpour, S., Javanmardi, A.: Multi-mode resource-constrained discrete time–cost-resource optimization in project scheduling using non-dominated sorting genetic algorithm. Automation in Construction 30, 216–227 (2013)
16. Sakellaropoulos, S., Chassiakos, A.P.: Project time–cost analysis under generalised precedence relations. Advances in Engineering Software 35(10-11), 715–724 (2004)
17. Hebert, J.E., Deckro, R.F.: Combining contemporary and traditional project management tools to resolve a project scheduling problem. Computers & Operations Research 38(1), 21–32 (2011)
18. Goldberg, D.E.: Genetic Algorithms in Search, Optimization, and Machine Learning. Addison-Wesley, Boston (1989)
19. University Partnership Programme, http://www.upp-ltd.com/university/exeter/ (accessed on June 05, 2013)
20. University Business, http://www.universitybusiness.co.uk/?q=news/university-exeter-and-upp-%C2%A3150m-deal/879 (accessed on June 05, 2013)
21. Savić, D.A., Bicik, J., Morley, M.S.: A DSS generator for multiobjective optimisation of spreadsheet-based models. Environmental Modelling Software 26(5), 551–561 (2011)

An Integrative Knowledge Management Framework to Support ERP Implementation for Improved Management Decision Making in Industry

Uchitha Jayawickrama, Shaofeng Liu, and Melanie Hudson Smith

School of Management, University of Plymouth, Plymouth, United Kingdom
{uchitha.jayawickrama,shaofeng.liu,
melanie.hudson-smith}@plymouth.ac.uk

Abstract. Knowledge Management (KM) has been identified as one of the key success factors for Enterprise Resource Planning (ERP) implementation and has received considerable academic attention in the last decade, whilst continuously gaining interest from industry. KM for ERP implementation is, however, a challenging task because of the complexity of ERP packages used in various industrial contexts. If implemented successfully, ERP systems will improve management decision making by providing more accurate, timely and integrated enterprise wide information. This study proposes an integrative KM competence (IKMC) framework that can provide holistic consideration of different types of knowledge across its life cycle phases. The framework has been tested with companies in service industry which have implemented standard ERP packages. The key findings indicate how to advance KM competence by knowledge creation, transfer, retention and application. In addition, the study informs practitioners about the most important knowledge types (ERP package and business process knowledge) and how, why and with what to create, transfer, retain and re-use knowledge during an ERP implementation to achieve project success.

Keywords: knowledge management competence, enterprise resource planning, integrative framework, management decision making.

1 Introduction

The global business environment has changed dramatically in recent years, as competition in complex knowledge based economies has increased. Enterprise Resource Planning (ERP) systems have been viewed as a way to manage increased business complexity, leading to the rapid adoption and implementation of such systems, as ERP can support enterprises to improve decision making performance [1, 2]. ERP is a strategic decision support tool that helps a company to gain competitive advantage by integrating business processes and optimising the resources available [3]. Over the past two decades, ERP systems have become one of the most important implementations in the corporate use of information technology. ERP implementations are usually large, complex projects, involving large groups of people and other resources, working collaboratively under considerable time pressure and facing many unforeseen developments [4, 5].

J.E. Hernández et al. (Eds.): EWG-DSS 2012, LNBIP 164, pp. 86–101, 2013.
© Springer-Verlag Berlin Heidelberg 2013

More recently, knowledge management (KM) has emerged as a discrete area in the study of organisations, to the extent that it has become recognized as a significant source of competitive advantage [6]. Effectively implementing a sound KM strategy and becoming a knowledge-based company is seen as a mandatory condition of success for organizations as they enter the era of the knowledge economy [7]. ERP systems are expected to reduce costs. by improving efficiencies through process advancements and enhance decision making by providing more accurate and timely enterprise wide integrated information [8]. The prospect of synergies between KM and ERP areas makes it an attractive area for current research, using KM to help face the challenge of increasing the success rate of ERP and reducing the risk of the implementation. Hence, this paper proposes an integrative KM competence framework for ERP success is reviewed in Section 2. Section 3 proposes an integrative KM competence framework and examines its main components. Thereafter and investigates the applicability of the framework in practice to guide future ERP implementations in industrial context towards success by increasing KM competence.

The rest of the paper is organised as follows: relevant literature on KM and ERP implementation, data collection approach together with data analysis and findings are presented in Sections 2, 3 and 4. Section 5 provides further discussion on the framework. Finally, management implications, limitations and further research are considered in the Conclusion section.

2   Relevant Literature

The majority of research in ERP system implementation is focused on critical success factors, critical failure factors, risk factors and effective factors relating to ERP implementations [9-15]. However, there are relatively few studies which specifically focus on knowledge management competence for ERP implementation success. This section mainly discusses the various KM and ERP implementation related literature.

Vandaie [16] identifies two major areas of concern regarding the management of knowledge in ERP projects through the developed framework; managing tacit knowledge and issues concerning the process-based nature of organizational knowledge. Furthermore, he identifies that facilitators are able to moderate these negative effects. The structure of team interactions and the atmosphere of the team help to moderate negative effects that are due to the tacit nature of ERP knowledge. Similarly, powerful core ERP teams and hiring in external consultants help to moderate the negative effects of the process-based nature of ERP knowledge and organisational memory. This study discusses two major barriers in knowledge creation and transfer in ERP projects and ways to mitigate them.

There is a large, significant and positive relationship between knowledge management competence and enterprise success, according to the quantitative study by Sedera and Gable [17]. The proposed model also demonstrates the equal importance of the four phases of the KM competence i.e. creation, transfer, retention and application. Furthermore, Sedera, Gable and Chan [18], Gable, Sedera and Chan [19] revealed that information quality, system quality, individual impact and organizational impact as variables in order to measure ERP success. The higher the organisation's level of enterprise system (ES) related KM competence; the higher the level of success of the ES will be [17]. Moreover, they explain almost half of the variance in ES success; thereby study identifies KM competence as possibly the most important antecedent of success.

Jones, Cline and Ryan [5] examined eight dimensions of culture and their impact on how the ERP implementation team is able to effectively share knowledge during implementation. This study shows ways to overcome cultural barriers to knowledge sharing. Furthermore, it develops a model that demonstrates the link between the dimensions of culture, and knowledge sharing during ERP implementation.

Maditinos, Chatzoudes and Tsairidis [20] introduce a conceptual framework that investigates the way that human inputs are linked to communication effectiveness, conflict resolution and knowledge transfer. They also show the effect of the above factors on successful ERP implementation. Moreover, they find that knowledge transfer is positively related to user support and consultant support. These findings are largely based on the phases of knowledge management i.e. creation, transfer, retention and application.

O'Leary [21] investigates the use of KM to support ERP systems across the entire life cycle, with particular interest in case-based KM. Organisation culture, business framework, ERP package and project are the knowledge types identified by Alavi and Leidner [22]. This is the only study which considered most knowledge types (four) in one study in order to understand the knowledge management for ERP domain broader. Chen [23] divides empirical knowledge into four different layers of "know-what", "know-why", "know-how", and "know-with" in the conceptual model based on the empirical knowledge characterization. Liu et al. [24] presented a waste elimination model which comprises of four knowledge layers (know-what, know-how, know-why and know-with) and seven knowledge components (over production, waiting time, excessive processes, defectives, excessive inventory, excessive motion and excessive transport) in order to develop a knowledge-based decision making system to offer organisation-wide waste elimination guidance and recommendations in the electronics manufacturing industry.

The common feature of the past studies discussed in this section is that they explored knowledge types, knowledge layers and KM life cycle phases in isolation. None of the studies were able to explore the integrated effect of knowledge types, knowledge layers and KM life cycle phases for ERP implementation. Although effective KM has been identified as one of the key drivers for successful ERP implementations, there has been a significant shortage of empirical research on management of knowledge related to ERP implementation [25]. Understanding this, it is quite evident that KM competence for ERP success domain demands more research.

3   An Integrative Knowledge Management Competence (IKMC) Framework

An integrative framework has been proposed based on a comprehensive literature review on KM competence and ERP implementation and the research gap identified in this particular area. The integrative KM competence (IKMC) framework defines its key components (including k-types, k-layers and KM life cycle phases) and the relationships between the components, as shown in Figure 1.

A positive relationship between KM competence and ERP success (measured by information quality, system quality, individual impact and organizational impact) and the significant contribution towards KM competence by KM life cycle phases were incorporated to this framework. The four ERP implementation success measures can be elaborated as follows [17-19]. Individual impact is concerned with how ERP system has influenced user's individual capabilities and effectiveness on behalf of the organization. Organizational impact refers to impact of ERP system at the organizational level; namely improved organisational results and capabilities. Information quality is concerned with the quality of ERP system outputs: namely, the quality of the information the system produces in reports and on screen. System quality of the ERP system is concerned with how the system designs to capture data from a technical and design perspective. KM competence is defined for this study by considering literature as the effective management of relevant knowledge for successful implementation of the ERP system [17-19]. Moreover, KM competence investigates with the support of three main components; k-types, k-layers and KM life cycle (see Figure 1) which provide the integrative perspective for KM competence for ERP success. KM life cycle comprises of four phases according to many research studies [22, 26-32]. They are k-creation, k-transfer, k-retention and k-application. The ERP related knowledge is created with the interactions of project team members both client and vendor, then the created knowledge is transferred from one party to other, thereafter the transferred knowledge is retained with the use of various methods, finally retained knowledge is re-used when required during the implementation. The unique feature of this study is that it explores the integrated effect of k-types, k-layers and KM life cycle phases for ERP implementation success.

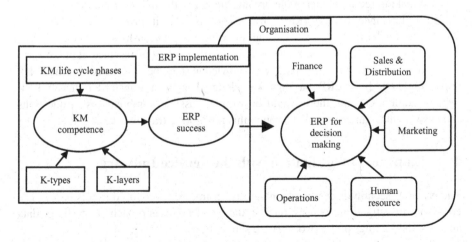

Fig. 1. Integrative KM Competence (IKMC) framework for ERP success

The k-types component considers four types of knowledge: ERP package knowledge, business process knowledge, organisational knowledge and project management knowledge [5, 20, 22, 33]. ERP package related knowledge explains as knowledge pertaining to features and functions of the system, business process related knowledge refers to As Is or existing process knowledge, Organisational cultural related knowledge explains the attitudes and behavioural aspect of the employees of an organisation, project management related knowledge refers to use of methodologies and approaches to manage the ERP implementation. The k-layers are comprised of know-what, know-how, know-why and know-with [23, 34]. Incorporating the k-layers component in the IKMC framework enables to discover what, how, why and with-what (ERP package, business process, organisational cultural and project management) knowledge have been created, transferred, retained and applied during ERP implementations.

An ERP system can be considered as a basic transactional system, which can be used for processing business transactions and as a management control system, which facilitates the planning and communication of business targets and goals [35]. Sammon, Adam and Carton [36] describe these 2 components of ERP systems as the solution to "operational" integration problems and "informational" requirements of managers. Nah, Lau and Kuang [9] expressed the same concepts by describing the use of information systems not only to automate manual tasks, but also to informate management tasks. ERP systems act as a decision support system and facilitate to make integrated decisions in functional areas of an organisation such as finance, operations, sales and distribution, human resource, marketing and so on [1, 9, 11, 13] (see Figure 1). However, ERP systems should be implemented correctly by effectively managing knowledge during the implementation in order to satisfy business needs and improve decision making performance [1, 2]. Hence, in the IKMC framework, ERP success measures have been used to achieve the enterprise wide decision making requirements of the organisation after the implementation.

The significance of the IKMC framework is that it provides an integrative perspective for KM competence through defining the relationships between its three main components i.e. k-types, k-layers and KM life cycle. For instance, it attempts to find out what sort of ERP package knowledge has been created during ERP implementation, how ERP package knowledge has been transferred during ERP implementation, etc. So, there would be various possible combinations of questions and answers that can be revealed through this integrative framework.

4   Empirical Investigation with the Service Industry

The previous section discusses the integrative framework proposed in this paper. The empirical investigation focuses on the data collection approach as well as data analysis and findings under two separate sub sections.

4.1   Data Collection Approach

Insightful interview has been used as the main approach for data collection from industry. The face-to-face, in-depth interviews have been chosen over other data collection methods mainly because they provide the ability to gather rich and detailed responses for what, how, why and with what, the four types of knowledge have been created, transferred, retained and applied during ERP implementation [6, 37, 38]. There are criteria for selecting suitable interview participants from the companies as nature of the research demands [5, 39] and the developed criteria for this study are as follows; participant should have directly involved with the standard ERP system (SAP, Oracle, JD Edwards, MS Dynamics, etc, not in-house developed systems) implementation at the case company and should have at least 10 years of ERP systems experience in UK. The integrative KM competence framework has been tested in the service industry. Table 1 illustrates the background of the ERP implementation of three companies (X, Y and Z) ranging from small, medium and large size.

Table 1. Background of the companies of small, medium and large size

Company	Business area	ERP package	Number of modules	Implementation duration	Number of employees/ active ERP users
Company X	Music	Oracle	18 modules	3.5 years	160 / 120
Company Y	Market Research	Oracle	10 modules	1.5 years	1500 / 1500
Company Z	Broadcasting	Oracle	12 modules	1.5 years	5000 / 5000

Even the size of the three companies are different, all of them have implemented the same ERP package (Oracle), there have not been any package specific features affect the findings of the study. Almost all employees are using the system which shows that enterprise wide decision making requirements have been satisfied by the ERP system itself. The implementation duration mainly depends on the number of modules and customisation efforts in order to facilitate specific business requirements in each business area. Each interview participant had direct work experience on ERP implementations for more than 15 years which shows the high level of skills and experience in ERP domain. They all have ERP implementation experience in UK including the direct involvement of the respective implementation. Each company implementation has been investigated with three different sources of evidence: 6 hours of in-depth interviews in total, analysis of ERP project related documents, and validation of coded data with the respective companies. Moreover, an interview template has been developed in order to validate the links between the components and thereby find out the applicability of the IKMC framework in practice. The interview mainly comprised 4 groups of questions with regard to ERP package knowledge, business process knowledge, organisational cultural knowledge and project management knowledge. Semi-structured interviews were carried out with ERP experts in respective companies. The purpose of the research and the structure of the interview were briefed to the participants before commencing the interview session.

4.2   Data Analysis and Findings

In this section, four propositions have been formulated in order to assess the degree to which knowledge management competence influences ERP implementation success with respect to the k-types, k-layers and KM life cycle phases which can be seen in the integrative framework. Word for word interview transcripts and ERP project documents were analysed using thematic, comparative and content analysis methods [40-42]. The thematic analysis was used to allow new themes to emerge from the transcripts and documents, whilst comparative and content analysis methods have been used to confirm the set of themes those were there before commencing the coding [41, 42], themes such as what, how and why different types of knowledge have been created, transferred, retained and applied during implementation. Furthermore, comparative analysis was used to confirm findings across 3 companies. The data analysis process is comprised of 3 steps: it identifies what, how, why and with-what the knowledge is created, transferred, retained and applied in step 1. In step 2, it categorises all knowledge activities under main four knowledge types. In step 3, it derives the key findings based on the frequent of occurrence of knowledge activities in 3 implementations. The k-layers (what, how, why, with) have been used to reveal the importance of four k-types in different KM life cycle phases and thereby produced the research findings with the integrated effects of k-layers, k-types and KM life cycle phases. The four propositions are discussed with evidence from the case companies based on 3 implementations which have been carried out in company X, company Y and company Z.

Proposition 1: The management of ***ERP package knowledge*** with the support of KM life cycle phases to achieve ERP success.

Proposition 2: The management of ***business process knowledge*** with the support of KM life cycle phases to achieve ERP success.

Proposition 3: The management of ***organisational cultural knowledge*** with the support of KM life cycle phases to achieve ERP success.

Proposition 4: The management of ***project management knowledge*** with the support of KM life cycle phases to achieve ERP success.

The summary of key findings can be seen in Table 2; it shows that ERP package and business process knowledge have been managed formally through the KM life cycle phases, but there is not much evidence of managing organisational cultural and project management knowledge formally through KM life cycle phases.

Table 2. Summary of key findings

The findings have been revealed
through k-layers (what, how, why, with)

K-type	KM life cycle phases:			
	K-creation	**K-transfer**	**K-retention**	**K-application**
ERP package Knowledge	Client and vendor project teams should be in one physical location (on-shore) to experience smooth knowledge creation between individuals.	Main ERP package related knowledge transfer methods are workshops, training sessions, piloting the system and UAT (user acceptance test).	There are few ways of retaining ERP package related knowledge such as documentation, help desk activities, handovers and buddy systems.	Quality of documentation determines the knowledge application during the implementation.
	Online KM systems managed by vendors determines the ERP package knowledge creation mainly in the latter stage of the implementation.	Use of train the trainer approach during implementations.	Documentation or practice of document management is the commonly used method.	
	Informal conversations also support for knowledge creation along with formal project meetings and brainstorming sessions.	The organisation structure sees as a determinant for k-transfer during ERP implementation.		
Business process Knowledge	Business process related knowledge has been created mainly through the super users.	The super users mainly take the lead to transfer current business process knowledge to consultants with the support of other users.	The main approach of retaining business process related knowledge is with As Is process documents.	The As Is process documents mainly use to plan data migrations and in customisations.
	It is vital to know the As Is process in order to determine the To Be process.	Effective knowledge transfer is determined by the knowledge absorption capability of the consultant/user.	Higher the customisations, higher the time and effort put to prepare As Is documents to a greater detail.	
Org. Cultural Knowledge	A consultant's previous implementation experience in a similar industry matters a lot to identify and adapt to the culture of the client organisation.			
	There have been difficulties in taking process information out of users during business requirement gathering discussions.			
	Companies deal with organisation cultural related activities then and there without attempting to retain that knowledge, since it is difficult to codify that knowledge.			
Project Management Knowledge	ERP implementations are run by the vendor itself and client's project manager does only the facilitation.			
	Project managers appointed by the client companies are with no prior ERP knowledge.			
	It is pointless to codify and retain the project management knowledge in order to build up that knowledge and expertise within the client company.			

Proposition 1: *The management of* **ERP package knowledge** *with the support of KM life cycle phases to achieve ERP success.*

Knowledge creation phase

The individual and organisational knowledge about a new ERP system starts from zero and it grows with the implementation. Regardless of a vanilla implementation or replacement, active participation of consultants is vital for ERP package related knowledge creation [20]. Therefore, client and vendor project teams should be together in one particular physical location in order to experience a smooth knowledge creation between individuals during an implementation. Furthermore, client and vendor teams should be merged together in such a way that one consultant works with one super user depending on the stage of the implementation. The off-shore (client and vendor project teams work remotely) work method has not materialised expected knowledge creation. However, depending on the individual consultant's attitude and positive or negative work relationship with the client project team members, some tend to share most of the knowledge with the client, but some not. The online KM systems managed by vendors determines the creation of ERP package knowledge not necessarily in the beginning but towards the latter stage of the implementation. Oracle has their own online knowledge base called Metalink (My Oracle Support), which comprises thousands of knowledge elements pertaining to Oracle ERP. Moreover, ERP package related knowledge such as functions and features of the system has been created during formal project meetings and brainstorming sessions [43]. The knowledge creation has happened during many informal chats, for an instance project related issues being discussed in corridors and social occasions. At that time the discussion mostly shifts to a different level. So users tend to discuss an issue in detail, which they could not do during the meeting because of shyness or unwillingness to go against the boss, or any other reason. But they might be more open when it comes to informal chats, although it would be very difficult to codify that knowledge in full [16]. However, as a result, a summary of the issue that has been discussed in the corridor or social occasion might go to formal records if it is worked out.

Knowledge transfer phase

The main ERP package related knowledge transfer methods are workshops, training sessions, piloting the system and UAT (user acceptance test) according to findings. When the UAT stage comes many users have forgotten what they have learnt during training sessions, because they are normally busy with day to day office work. So, they learn a great deal about the ERP system during UAT because users should provide sign offs for UAT scripts. It forces them to grab the knowledge of the system willingly or unwillingly. Therefore, UAT becomes a determinant for k-transfer as far as ERP package knowledge is concerned. Furthermore, training sessions can be conducted internally for all users of the system, mostly conducted during the implementation by the vendor and also the client organisation can send selected users or super users for external intensive training to the vendor. Many companies use a train the trainer approach in educating other users who could not attend training sessions. This shows how, why and with what ERP package knowledge has been transferred at respective stages of the implementation. In addition, project team members should be selected correctly for the implementation from the client company [5]. They are called key or super users. They have detailed knowledge of the business processes and will be appointed by the respective departments/functions. Super users should be responsible of facilitating smooth knowledge transfer between consultants to end users and vice versa [20]. Moreover, organisation structure is seen as a determinant for k-transfer during ERP implementation. The client company should compare the existing organisational structure with the To Be structure after the system implementation, thereby identifying the roles and responsibilities of the employees and start transferring adequate knowledge to the correct employee from the beginning.

Knowledge retention phase

There are few ways of retaining ERP package related knowledge such as documentation, help desk activities, handovers and buddy systems. Documentation or practice of document management is the most commonly used method [44]. Documents are in a few types such as process documents, setup documents, technical documents and training manuals. The case companies mainly used a shared drive on the network to store documents for re-use during the implementation. Documents were updated frequently, versioned and given access for relevant users. If there are many customisations, the company should retain existing employees who were there during the implementation, because they are the only people who know about the changes did to the standard system in detail in order to operate and maintain the system. Moreover, clients tend to maintain documents according to vendor's document configuration methods. For instance Oracle consultants use AIM (application implementation methodology) as implementation methodology and it contains a way of configuring implementation related documents with specific formats.

Knowledge application phase

It is important to pick the knowledge at the beginning and pass it all through the ERP implementation cycle. The solution design documents have been used during the UAT stage and interface development stage, this implies that clients require the knowledge that they created, transferred and retained at the beginning of the implementation in order to accomplish tasks in middle and latter stages of the implementation. Hence, the quality of documentation determines the application of relevant knowledge during implementation. Documents produced during the implementation should be accurate and up-to-date; otherwise usage of the same will lead the implementation to failure.

The ERP package knowledge helps users to move from data entry person to analytical person. As the awareness and knowledge about the ERP system increases, integrated and accurate information can be pulled from various types of reports and screens to make effective management decisions. Thereby, it improves organisational results and capabilities by reducing costs and maximising profits. In summary, ERP package related knowledge would increase the KM competence and it is fundamental and very important for ERP implementation success as far as four success measures are concerned.

*Proposition 2: The management of **business process knowledge** with the support of KM life cycle phases to achieve ERP success.*

Knowledge creation phase

The business process related knowledge refers to As Is or existing process related activities in an ERP implementation [22]. It is important to identify and draw the current business process in order to determine the To Be process or how it looks like after the implementation. Most business process related knowledge is created by users and then shared among the consultants to learn and understand the business of the client company.

Knowledge transfer phase

The super users mainly take the leadership to transfer current business process knowledge to consultants with the support of other users. Thereby, consultants understand the existing way of carrying out the business activities and start mapping these into ERP system features and functions [20]. Furthermore, super users mainly take the responsibility of generating the As Is process document and publish them back to the company in order to understand users and senior executives how the whole business is operating. In between above process, there are several feedback sessions with users to validate and check the accuracy of the As Is. Moreover, the receiver of knowledge that could be either a user or a consultant should have the capability of absorbing knowledge in the right quantities. Hence, knowledge absorption capacity would determine the effective knowledge transfer between individuals during the implementation [5]. On the other hand, knowledge should be transferred to the right person, at the right time and in correct quantity by the consultant and user. It can be evidently seen that how k-layers (i.e. why, how, what and with) integrate with business process knowledge in order to transfer knowledge during implementation.

Knowledge retention phase

The main approach of retaining business process related knowledge is with As Is process documents according to the findings. These documents can be split down by the departments and/or key process areas. The As Is documents are generated at a high level without going into much detail, when there are less customisations on the ERP system to meet business requirements. If the organisation is flexible enough to adopt the standard ERP functionalities by changing the existing business processes, then there is a high probability of implementing best business practices through the new implementation. Companies published the approved As Is documents on the shared drive like other project documents, so that users can access them and see that how particular individual's work relates to others tasks of the organisation.

Knowledge application phase

The As Is process documents are mainly used to plan data migrations and in customisations. They have also been useful during UAT stage and go-live, so that users could go back and see how they used to work before the new system was introduced and accordingly understand the system's way of performing tasks within their respective roles when providing sign-offs for UAT scripts. The findings shows that higher the customisations, higher the time and effort put to prepare As Is documents, because it requires knowledge of the current processes to a greater detail in order to plan and develop customisations.

The system quality is mainly depended on the way in which the system is configured by understanding existing business processes. Thereby, the system is enabled to capture relevant data for management decision making in various functional areas of the organisation. Also, proper understanding of As Is process is vital to retrieve accurate and integrated information which are produced in system generated reports and on various screens of the system. In conclusion, business process knowledge is necessary and it increases the KM competence of the organisation in collaboration with k-layers and KM life cycle phases to achieve ERP success.

Proposition 3: *The management of* **organisational cultural knowledge** *with the support of KM life cycle phases to achieve ERP success.*

A consultant's previous implementation experience in a similar industry matters a lot to identify and adapt to the culture of the client organisation. Moreover, there would be difficulties in taking information out of users during business requirement gathering discussions for various reasons such as fear of losing knowledge and power, resistance to the new system, etc, so it implies that project team should fight with own internal culture [33, 45]. On the other hand, battles between business and technical staff such as finalising customisation points and requirements are common during an implementation. Senior executives' interference in these situations is vital to direct them on correct path.

The impact from the organisation culture depends on how long the existing systems have been in place. Whatever system is implemented, at the end of the day it will be used by an individual with a set of attitudes towards the system and bound by the culture of the organisation [45]. Therefore, it is vital to pay attention to the culture the business operates in. However, organisational cultural knowledge resides in individual's minds and has not been codified through KM life cycle phases during ERP implementations. Companies deal with organisation cultural related activities then and there without attempting to retain that knowledge, since it is difficult to codify that knowledge. However, it can be seen that how and why (k-layers) organisational cultural knowledge is important to achieve ERP implementation success.

Proposition 4: *The management of* **project management knowledge** *with the support of KM life cycle phases to achieve ERP success.*

The project management knowledge creation, transfer, retention and application occur informally most of the time during an implementation. The case companies were left with project plans, estimations and charts end of the implementation. Apart from that there has not been any codification of knowledge through KM life cycle phases [16]. Many of the implementations are run by the vendor itself and client's project manager does only the facilitation. Most of the project managers appointed by the client companies have no prior ERP knowledge. Therefore, clients heavily rely on the vendor for project management related activities [5]. Some believe that the fundamentals of a software project are the same; there will only be slight differences in estimations, resource requirements, etc. Even though they formally retain project management knowledge that would not be at least useful for ERP system upgrades according to the case companies.

The companies ranked the importance of knowledge types which would increase KM competence for ERP implementation success as shown in Table 3. Rank 1 to 4 from very important to least important.

Table 3. Ranking of knowledge types

Company K-type	X	Y	Z
ERP package K	1	1	1
Business process K	2	2	1
Org. Cultural K	2	4	4
Project Mgmt K	4	3	3

This implies that ERP package knowledge is the most important k-type and secondly business process knowledge. The organisational cultural and project management knowledge types are less important than other two. It reflects that in practice they perform formal knowledge creation, transfer, retention and application only as far as ERP package and business process k-types are concerned, but not with organisational cultural and project management knowledge types.

5   Discussion

Out of the four k-types, ERP package knowledge and business process knowledge have been extensively used and are relevant to industrial practices. The organisational cultural and project management knowledge have been less used in actual ERP implementations in order to increase KM competence of the organisation. This shows that research outcomes are partially in line with Alavi and Leidner [22] as far as k-types are concerned. Nevertheless, the four k-layers have shown the applicability to reveal the KM competence with the support of k-types and KM life cycle phases to achieve ERP success in service industry. K-layers were used by Chen [23] for IT industry in his study and through this research k-layers were used specifically to ERP context integrated with k-types and KM life cycle phases.

The four ERP success measures (system quality, information quality, individual impact and organisational impact) have been used to enable effective decision making in various functional areas of the organisation such as finance, marketing, human resource, operations and sales. Higher the level of As Is process knowledge and ERP package knowledge, higher the system quality and quality of the information that the system produces in reports and on screen for decision making. Therefore, individual capabilities and effectiveness on operational and managerial decision making have been improved through the new system implementation. Eventually, organisational results have also been increased in three business areas due to effective decision making of the employees through the ERP system.

The research reveals the integration of the three components i.e. k-types, k-layers and KM life cycle to build up KM competence within the organisation to achieve ultimate ERP implementation success, thereby, improving the decision making performance in various functional areas of the organisation. Moreover, this research shows the applicability of the IKMC framework in industrial real situations, which provides an integrative perspective on KM for the ERP implementation domain.

6   Conclusion

The research is important for industrial practitioners and academics in three main ways. Firstly it classifies key findings on knowledge creation, transfer, retention and application with respect to KM competence through the integrative framework. Therefore, practitioners can emphasise those key findings during ERP implementations. Secondly, it informs practitioners about the most important knowledge types (ERP package and business process knowledge) and how, why and with what to create, transfer, retain and re-use knowledge during an ERP implementation to achieve project success. Furthermore, they can prioritise and provide less attention on less important k-types. Thirdly, this is the first integrative framework that discovers what, how, why and with ERP package, business process, organisational cultural and project management knowledge have been created, transferred, retained and applied during ERP implementations. Thereby, this study adds new academic knowledge to KM and ERP domain. If implemented properly by considering these KM aspects, the ERP system should act as an integrated decision making system at all levels of the organisation.

Nevertheless, this research has some limitations; it focuses only on implementation, not pre or post implementation. Furthermore, the sample only covers Oracle ERP product implementations in UK service industry.

Further research will extend the IKMC framework to cover more standard ERP products in other regions apart from UK and extend the investigation to other industries such as manufacturing. Moreover, a quantitative survey will be carried out to find out the importance of k-types to increase KM competence with the links of k-layers and KM life cycle. Therefore, the applicability and validity of the framework can be generalised for more industrial contexts. Finally, the integrative framework will be extended for the pre and post implementation stages as well.

References

1. Davenport, T.H.: Putting the enterprise into the enterprise system. Harvard Business Review, 121–131 (July-August 1998)
2. Li, H., Li, L.: Integrating systems concepts into manufacturing information systems. Systems Research and Behavioral Science 17, 135–147 (2000)
3. O'Leary, D.E.: Enterprise Resource Planning System: Systems, Lifecycle, Electronic Commerce and Risk. Cambridge University Press, Cambridge (2000)
4. Kumar, K., van Hillegersberg, J.: Enterprise resource planning experiences and evolution. Communications of the ACM 43, 22–26 (2000)
5. Jones, M.C., Cline, M., Ryan, S.: Exploring knowledge sharing in ERP implementation, an organizational culture framework. Decision Support Systems 41, 411–434 (2006)

6. Kraemmerand, P., Møller, C., Boer, H.: ERP implementation: An integrated process of radical change and continuous learning. Production Planning & Control 14, 338–348 (2003)
7. Murray, P.: Knowledge management as a sustained competitive advantage. Ivey Business Journal 66, 71–76 (2002)
8. Poston, R., Grabski, S.: Financial impacts of enterprise resource planning implementations. International Journal of Accounting Information Systems, 271–294 (December 2001)
9. Nah, F., Lau, J., Kuang, J.: Critical factors for successful implementation of enterprise systems. Business Process Management Journal 7, 285–296 (2001)
10. Somers, T.M., Nelson, K.: The Impact of Critical Success Factors across the Stages of Enterprise Resource Planning Implementations. In: Proceedings of the 34th Hawaii International Conference on System Sciences (HICSS) (2001)
11. Huang, S., Chang, I., Li, S., Lin, M.: Assessing risk in ERP projects: identify and prioritize the factors. Industrial Management & Data Systems 104, 681–688 (2004)
12. Wong, A., Scarbrough, H., Chau, P., Davison, R.: Critical Failure Factors in ERP Implementation. In: Proceedings of the Ninth Pacific Asia Conference on Information Systems (PACIS) (2005)
13. Upadhyay, P., Jahanyan, S., Dan, P.: Factors influencing ERP implementation in Indian manufacturing organizations. Journal of Enterprise Information Management 24, 130–145 (2011)
14. Al-Turki, U.M.: An exploratory study of ERP implementation in Saudi Arabia. Production Planning & Control 22, 403–413 (2011)
15. Dey, P.K., Clegg, B., Cheffi, W.: Risk management in enterprise resource planning implementation: a new risk assessment framework. Production Planning & Control, 1–14 (2011)
16. Vandaie, R.: The role of organizational knowledge management in successful ERP implementation projects. Knowledge-Based Systems 21, 920–926 (2008)
17. Sedera, D., Gable, G.: Knowledge management competence for enterprise system success. Journal of Strategic Information Systems 19, 296–306 (2010)
18. Sedera, D., Gable, G., Chan, T.: Knowledge management for ERP success. In: Pacific Asia Conference on Information Systems (2003)
19. Gable, G.G., Sedera, D., Chan, T.: Re-conceptualizing Information System Success: The IS-Impact Measurement Model. Journal of the Association for Information Systems 9, 377–408 (2008)
20. Maditinos, D., Chatzoudes, D., Tsairidis, C.: Factors affecting ERP system implementation effectiveness. Journal of Enterprise Information Management 25, 60–78 (2012)
21. O'Leary, D.E.: Knowledge management across the enterprise resource planning systems life cycle. International Journal of Accounting Information Systems 3, 99–110 (2002)
22. Alavi, M., Leidner, D.: Review: knowledge management and knowledge management systems: conceptual foundations and research issues. MIS Quarterly (MISQ Review) 25, 107–136 (2001)
23. Chen, Y.-J.: Development of a method for ontology-based empirical knowledge representation and reasoning. Decision Support Systems 50, 1–20 (2010)
24. Liu, S., Annansingh, F., Moizer, J., Liu, L., Sun, W.: A knowledge system for integrated production waste elimination in support of organisational decision making. In: Hernández, J.E., Zarate, P., Dargam, F., Delibašić, B., Liu, S., Ribeiro, R. (eds.) EWG-DSS 2011. LNBIP, vol. 121, pp. 134–150. Springer, Heidelberg (2012)

25. Gable, G.: The enterprise system lifecycle: through a knowledge management lens. Strategic Change 14, 255–263 (2005)
26. Huber, G.P.: Organizational Learning: The Contributing Processes and the Literatures. Organization Science 2, 88–115 (1991)
27. Stein, E.W., Zwass, V.: Actualizing Organizational Memory with Information Systems. Information Systems Research 6, 85–117 (1995)
28. Szulanski, G.: Exploring Internal Stickiness: Impediments to the Transfer of Best Practice within the Firm. Strategic Management Journal 17, 27–43 (1996)
29. Bartezzaghi, E., Corso, M., Verganti, R.: Continuous Improvement and Inter-Project Learning in New Product Development. International Journal of Technology Management 14, 116–138 (1997)
30. Wiig, K.M.: Knowledge Management: Where Did it Come From and Where will it Go. Journal of Expert Systems with Applications 13, 1–14 (1997)
31. Argote, L.: Organizational Learning: Creating, Retaining and Transferring Knowledge. Kluwer Academic Publishers, Boston (1999)
32. Horwitch, M., Armacost, R.: Helping Knowledge Management Be all it Can Be. Journal of Business Strategy 23, 26–31 (2002)
33. Hung, W.-H., Ho, C.-F., Jou, J.-J., Kung, K.-H.: Relationship bonding for a better knowledge transfer climate: An ERP implementation research. Decision Support Systems 52, 406–414 (2012)
34. Liu, S., Leat, M., Moizer, J., Megicks, P., Kasturiratne, D.: A decision-focused knowledge management framework to support collaborative decision making for lean supply chain management. International Journal of Production Research 51(7), 2123–2137 (2012)
35. Carton, F., Adam, F.: Understanding the Impact of Enterprise Systems on Management Decision Making: An Agenda for Future Research. The Electronic Journal of Information Systems Evaluation 8, 99–106 (2005)
36. Sammon, D., Adam, F., Carton, F.: The Realities of Benefit Realisation in the Monolithic Enterprise Systems Era- Considerations for the Future. In: Proceedings of the 10th European Conference on Information Technology Evaluation (2003)
37. Baskerville, R., Pawlowski, S., McLean, E.: Enterprise resource planning and organizational knowledge: patterns of convergence and divergence. In: International Conference on Information Systems (2000)
38. McAdam, R., Galloway, A.: Enterprise resource planning and organisational innovation: a management perspective. Industrial Management & Data Systems 105, 280–290 (2005)
39. Newell, S., Huang, J.C., Galliers, R.D., Pan, S.L.: Implementing enterprise resource planning and knowledge management systems in tandem, fostering efficiency and innovation complementarity. Information & Organisation 13, 25–52 (2003)
40. Miles, M.B., Huberman, A.M.: An Expanded Sourcebook Qualitative Data Analysis. Sage Publications, California (1994)
41. Dawson, C.: Practical Research Methods. How to Books, Oxford (2002)
42. Tharenou, P., Donohue, R., Cooper, B.: Management Research Methods. Cambridge University Press, New York (2007)
43. Xu, L., Wang, C., Luo, X., Shi, Z.: Integrating knowledge management and ERP in enterprise information systems. Systems Research and Behavioral Science 23, 147–156 (2006)
44. Tsai, M.-T., Li, E.Y., Lee, K.-W., Tung, W.-H.: Beyond ERP implementation: the moderating effect of knowledge management on business performance. Total Quality Management & Business Excellence 22, 131–144 (2011)
45. Donate, M.J., Guadamillas, F.: Organizational factors to support knowledge management and innovation. Journal of Knowledge Management 15, 890–914 (2011)

A Web-Based Decision Support System Using Basis Update on Simplex Type Algorithms

Nikolaos Ploskas*, Nikolaos Samaras, and Jason Papathanasiou

University of Macedonia, 156 Egnatia Str., Thessaloniki 54006, Greece
{ploskas,samaras,jasonp}@uom.gr

Abstract. Linear Programming is a significant and well-studied optimization methodology. Simplex type algorithms have been widely used in Decision Support Systems. The computation of the basis inverse is a crucial step in simplex type algorithms. In this paper, we review and compare three basis update methods. We incorporate these methods on the exterior and the revised simplex algorithm in order to highlight the significance of the choice of the basis update method in simplex type algorithms and the reduction that can offer to the solution time. We perform a computational comparison in which the basis inverse is computed with three updating methods. Finally, we have implemented a web-based Decision Support System that assists decision makers in the selection of the algorithm and basis update method in order to solve their Linear Programming problems.

Keywords: Linear Programming, Decision Support System, Exterior Point Simplex Algorithm, Revised Simplex Algorithm, Basis Inverse.

1 Introduction

Web-based Decision Support Systems (DSS) are computerized information systems that support decision-policy makers using a Web browser [20]. The three most widely used frameworks for implementing web-based DSS are communication-driven, knowledge-driven and document-driven DSS [3]. Communication-driven DSS bring together multiple decision makers using electronic communication technologies. Communication-driven DSS may also assist managers in collaborative decision-making processes (for more information, see [10]). Knowledge-driven DSS recommend actions to decision makers. Finally, document-driven DSS support managers organize and analyze large volumes of data.

Web-based DSS can be implemented using three different Web technologies [2]: (i) server-side technologies, (ii) client-side technologies, and (iii) distributed implementations. Server-side technologies include Java applications, ASP, PHP, CGI, and JSP, while client-side tecnologies include Java applets and ActiveX controls. Finally, distributed implementations are based on Java RMI, COM+, and Enterprise Java Beans. Recently, DSS also utilize web services and messaging protocols like SOAP [3].

---

* Corresponding author.

J.E. Hernández et al. (Eds.): EWG-DSS 2012, LNBIP 164, pp. 102–114, 2013.

This paper presents a web-based knowledge-driven DSS that supports decision makers solving their Linear Programming problems. Operations research applications that the proposed DSS can be utilized include telecommunications, bio-informatics, revenue management, supply chain management, resource allocation, etc. A real application case study for the transition from fossil to renewable energy resources in the United States [11] adapted from Manne [15] is presented in Section 5, in which our application can be utilized in the decision making process. The user interface of the proposed DSS has been implemented using jsp, while the simplex type algorithms have been implemented with MATLAB.

The structure of the paper is as follows. Section 2 presents the background of our work. Section 3 includes the presentation of the three basis update methods, while in Section 4 the computational experiments are presented. In Section 5, a web-based DSS for the selection of the algorithm and basis update method is presented. Finally, the conclusions of this paper are outlined in Section 6.

2   Background

Linear Programming (LP) is the process of minimizing or maximizing a linear objective function $z = \sum_{j=1}^{n} c_j x_j$ to a number of linear equality and inequality constraints. The simplex algorithm is the most widely used method for solving Linear Programming problems (LPs). Consider the following LP (LP.1) in the standard form:

$$
\begin{aligned}
min \quad & c^T x \\
s.t. \quad & Ax = b \\
& x \geq 0
\end{aligned}
\qquad (LP.1)
$$

where $A \in \mathbb{R}^{m \times n}$, $(c, x) \in \mathbb{R}^n$, $b \in \mathbb{R}^m$, and T denotes transposition. We assume that A has full rank, $rank(A) = m, m < n$. Consequently, the linear system $Ax = b$ is consistent. The simplex algorithm searches for an optimal solution by moving from one feasible solution to another, along the edges of the feasible set. The dual problem associated with the (LP.1) is presented in (DP.1):

$$
\begin{aligned}
min \quad & b^T w \\
s.t. \quad & A^T w + s = c \\
& s \geq 0
\end{aligned}
\qquad (DP.1)
$$

where $w \in \mathbb{R}^m$ and $s \in \mathbb{R}^n$.

Using a partition (B, N) (LP.1) can be written as follows:

$$min \quad c_B^T x_B + c_N^T x_N$$
$$s.t. \ A_B x_B + A_N x_N = b \qquad (LP.2)$$
$$x_B, x_N \geq 0$$

In the above problem, A_B is an $m \times m$ non-singular submatrix of A, called basic matrix or basis. The columns of A belonging to subset B are called basic and those belonging to N are called non basic. The solution of the linear problem $x_B = (A_B)^{-1} b, x_N = 0$ is called a basic solution. A solution $x = (x_B, x_N)$ is feasible iff $x \geq 0$; otherwise, the solution is infeasible. The solution of the (DP.1) is computed by the relation $s = c - A^T w$, where $w = (c_B)^T (A_B)^{-1}$ are the simplex multipliers and s are the dual slack variables. The basis A_B is dual feasible iff $s \geq 0$.

In each iteration, the simplex algorithm interchanges a column of matrix A_B with a column of matrix A_N and constructs a new basis $A_{\overline{B}}$. Any iteration of simplex type algorithms is relatively expensive. The total execution time of an iteration of simplex type algorithms is dictated by the computation of the basis inverse. This inverse, however, does not have to be computed from scratch during each iteration of the simplex algorithm. Simplex type algorithms maintain a factorization of basis and update this factorization in each iteration. This step must be carefully designed and implemented, because it is the most time-consuming step in simplex-type algorithms. Many updating methods have been proposed [1][4][6][7][16][21][22]. In Section 2 we present three well-known methods for the basis inverse.

Simplex type algorithms have been widely used in Decision Support Systems. Ghodsypour and O'Brien [9] have implemented a DSS for supplier selection using the revised simplex method. Lappi et al. [12] designed an information system for forest management planning systems which generate alternative treatment schedules for treatment units and select optimal schedule combinations using the simplex method. Venkataramanan and Bornstein [23] have proposed a network-based DSS for the assigning parking spaces utilizing primal network simplex algorithm. Lauer et al. [13] have implemented a DSS to schedule student computer lab attendants at a major university using the revised simplex algorithm. Lourenço et al. [14] have proposed a DSS for portfolio robustness evaluation using a solver based on the revised simplex algorithm.

In a previous paper [19], we reviewed and compared both the CPU- and GPU-based implementations of five updating methods, namely: (i) Gaussian Elimination, (ii) the built-in function inv of MATLAB, (iii) LU decomposition, (iv) Product Form of the Inverse (PFI) and (v) a Modification of the Product Form of the Inverse (MPFI); and incorporated them with the revised simplex algorithm. We have performed a computational study over dense randomly optimal generated LPs and concluded that MPFI, PFI and MATLAB's inv are the best serial basis update methods. In this paper, a computational study is performed in order to highlight the impact of the choice of the basis update methods on the exterior and the revised simplex algorithm. The Exterior Primal Simplex Algorithm (EPSA) that we used has been proposed by Paparrizos et al. [18]. This algorithm outperforms the Revised Simplex Method (RSM) as the problem size increases and the density decreases. The RSM in the computational study has been proposed by Dantzig [5].

3 Basis Update Methods

In this section, three widely-used updating methods are presented: (i) the MATLAB's built-in method inv, (ii) the Product Form of the Inverse, and (iii) the Modification of the Product Form of the Inverse.

3.1 MATLAB's Built-In Function inv

MATLAB's built-in function inv can be used to compute the basis inverse in every step of the algorithms. MATLAB's inv uses LAPACK routines to compute the basis inverse and is already optimized. Hence, its execution time is smaller compared with other relevant methods that compute the explicit basis inverse. The time complexity of this method is $O(n^3)$.

3.2 Product Form of the Inverse

The new basis inverse can be updated, according to the PFI updating method [6], at any iteration using the equation (1):

$$(A_{\overline{B}})^{-1} = (A_B E)^{-1} = E^{-1}(A_B)^{-1} \tag{1}$$

where E^{-1} is the inverse of the eta-matrix and can be computed by (2).

$$E^{-1} = I - \frac{1}{h_{rl}}(h_l - e_l)e_l^T = \begin{bmatrix} 1 & & -h_{1l} & \\ & \ddots & \vdots & \\ & & 1/h_{rl} & \\ & & \vdots & \ddots \\ & & -h_{ml}/h_{rl} & & 1 \end{bmatrix} \tag{2}$$

If the current basis inverse is computed using regular multiplication, then the complexity of the PFI is $\Theta(m^3)$.

3.3 A Modification of Product Form of the Inverse

In MPFI updating scheme [4], the current basis inverse $(A_{\overline{B}})^{-1}$ can be computed from the previous inverse $(A_B)^{-1}$ using a simple outer product of two vectors and one matrix addition, as shown in the equation (3):

$$(A_{\overline{B}})^{-1} = \left(A_{\overline{B}_{r.}}\right)^{-1} + v \otimes (A_{B_{r.}})^{-1} \tag{3}$$

The updating scheme of the inverse is shown in (4).

$$(A_{\overline{B}})^{-1} = \begin{vmatrix} b_{11} & \cdots & b_{1m} \\ \vdots & \ddots & \vdots \\ 0 & 0 & 0 \\ \vdots & \ddots & \vdots \\ b_{m1} & \cdots & b_{mm} \end{vmatrix} + \begin{matrix} (A_B)^{-1} : \begin{vmatrix} b_{r1} & \cdots & b_{rr} & \cdots & b_{rm} \end{vmatrix} \\ \begin{vmatrix} -\frac{h_{1l}}{h_{rl}} \\ \vdots \\ -\frac{1}{h_{rl}} \\ \vdots \\ -\frac{h_{ml}}{h_{rl}} \end{vmatrix} \end{matrix} \tag{4}$$

The time complexity of this method is $\Theta(m^2)$.

4   Computational Study

A computational study of the aforementioned updating techniques on the EPSA and RSM is presented in this section. The computational comparison has been performed on a quad-processor Intel Core i7 3.4 GHz with 32 Gbyte of main memory and 8 cores, running under Microsoft Windows 7 64-bit. The algorithms have been implemented using MATLAB Professional R2013a.

The Netlib set of LPs [8] was used in this computational study, which is a well-known suite containing many read world LPs. 71% of the Netlib LPs are ill-conditioned [17], so numerical difficulties may occur. Table 1 presents some useful information about the test bed, which was used in the computational study. The first column includes the name of the problem, the second the number of constraints, the third the number of variables, the fourth the nonzero elements of matrix A and the fifth the objective value. For each instance, we averaged times over 10 runs.

In this computational study, we examine the significance of the choice of the basis updating technique on EPSA and RSM. Thus, we have executed these algorithms with the three different basis update methods presented in Section 2. Table 2 presents the results from the execution of EPSA and RSM with the aforementioned basis update methods over the Netlib set. All times in Table 2 are measured in seconds using the MATLAB's built-in command cputime. In Table 2, the following abbreviations are used: (i) INV - MATLAB's built-in function, (ii) PFI - Product Form of the Inverse, and (iii) MPFI - Modification of the Product Form of the Inverse. The results are graphically illustrated in Figure 1.

From the above results, we observe that: (i) the percentage of the time to compute the basis inverse to the total time is bigger in RSM than EPSA, and (ii) PFI is much faster than MPFI and MATLAB's inv over the Netlib set.

Table 1. Statistics of the Netlib LPs (optimal, Kennington and infeasible LPs)

Name	Constraints	Variables	Nonzeros A	Objective value
ADLITTLE	57	97	465	2.25E+05
AFIRO	28	32	88	-4.65E+02
AGG	489	163	2,541	-3.60E+07
AGG2	517	302	4,515	-2.02E+07
AGG3	517	302	4,531	1.03E+07
BANDM	306	472	2,659	-1.59E+02
BEACONFD	174	262	3,476	3.36E+04
BLEND	75	83	521	-3.08E+01
DEGEN2	445	534	4,449	-1.44E+03
E226	224	282	2,767	-1.88E+01
FFFFF800	525	854	6,235	5.56E+05
ISRAEL	175	142	2,358	-8.97E+05
LOTFI	154	308	1,086	-2.53E+01
SC50A	51	48	131	-6.46E+01
SC50B	51	48	119	-7.00E+01
SC105	106	103	281	-5.22E+01
SC205	206	203	552	-5.22E+01
SCAGR7	130	140	553	-2.33E+06
SCFXM1	331	457	2,612	1.84E+04
SCFXM2	661	914	5,229	3.67E+04
SCFXM3	991	1,371	7,846	5.49E+04
SCORPION	389	358	1708	1.88E+03
SCRS8	491	1,169	4,029	9.04E+02
SCTAP1	301	480	2,052	1.41E+03
SCTAP3	1,481	2,480	10,734	1.42E+03
SHARE1B	118	225	1,182	-7.66E+04
SHARE2B	97	79	730	-4.16E+02
SHIP04L	403	2,118	8,450	1.79E+06
SHIP04S	403	1,458	5,810	1.80E+06
SHIP08L	779	4,283	17,085	1.91E+06
SHIP08S	779	2,387	9,501	1.92E+06
SHIP12L	1,152	5,427	21,597	1.47E+06
SHIP12S	1,152	2,763	10,941	1.49E+06
STOCFOR1	118	111	474	-4.11E+04

5   Decision Support System Analysis and Design

5.1   Object-Oriented Analysis

Figure 2 presents the decision making process that the decision-policy maker can perform using the DSS. Firstly, decision maker formulates the problem under examination as a linear programming problem. Then, the data acquisition,

Table 2. Results of the Exterior and the Revised Simplex Algorithm Using Three Different Updating Methods over the Netlib Set)

Name	EPSA-INV		EPSA-PFI		EPSA-MPFI		RSM-INV		RSM-PFI		RSM-MPFI	
	Total	Inverse	Total	Inverse	Total	Inverse	Total	Inverse	Total	Inverse	Total	Inverse
ADLITTLE	0.1872	0.0653	0.1746	0.0362	0.1544	0.0377	0.0936	0.0468	0.0312	0.0020	0.0468	0.0312
AFIRO	0.0312	0.0123	0.0162	0.0042	0.0268	0.0050	0.0010	0.0001	0.0010	0.0001	0.0010	0.0001
AGG	0.1092	0.0468	0.0772	0.0179	0.0932	0.0190	0.3432	0.2496	0.0780	0.0312	0.0936	0.0468
AGG2	0.2808	0.0312	0.2317	0.0176	0.2642	0.0187	1.0140	0.8736	0.2184	0.0780	0.2496	0.0624
AGG3	0.3432	0.0468	0.1647	0.0265	0.3193	0.0276	1.5912	1.4040	0.2652	0.0936	0.2652	0.1248
BANDM	0.7176	0.1716	0.6816	0.0885	0.6943	0.0948	1.7160	1.2012	0.6552	0.1404	0.6552	0.1560
BEACONFD	0.0312	0.0153	0.0280	0.0094	0.0219	0.0108	0.0312	0.0230	0.0312	0.0020	0.0156	0.0050
BLEND	0.0936	0.0780	0.0681	0.0425	0.0782	0.0507	0.0780	0.0624	0.0312	0.0156	0.0312	0.0016
DEGEN2	5.2884	2.9172	3.1063	1.8425	3.4833	2.072	17.0509	15.4285	5.7408	3.8844	6.4428	4.5864
E226	0.4056	0.1716	0.2470	0.1101	0.2967	0.1256	1.2324	1.1544	0.2808	0.2028	0.2496	0.1404
FFFFF800	1.2792	0.2496	0.7301	0.1408	0.9131	0.1497	1.9032	1.0608	1.1232	0.2808	1.1232	0.2808
ISRAEL	0.1404	0.0468	0.1081	0.0238	0.1189	0.0266	0.5616	0.5460	0.1092	0.0624	0.0936	0.0624
LOTFI	0.2496	0.0312	0.1869	0.0171	0.2117	0.0203	0.3276	0.1716	0.1716	0.0468	0.1716	0.0468
SC50A	0.0936	0.0624	0.0616	0.0341	0.0622	0.0364	0.0936	0.0780	0.0624	0.0030	0.0312	0.005
SC50B	0.6396	0.4836	0.4236	0.1847	0.4633	0.2048	0.5304	0.4056	0.2184	0.1092	0.1872	0.0780
SC105	0.0312	0.0156	0.0243	0.0083	0.0234	0.0088	0.0468	0.0034	0.0312	0.0020	0.0156	0.0050
SC205	0.0156	0.0068	0.0094	0.0032	0.0127	0.0036	0.0312	0.0180	0.0156	0.0020	0.0000	0.0030
SCAGR7	0.0936	0.0312	0.0618	0.0156	0.0782	0.0182	0.0936	0.0560	0.0780	0.0156	0.0780	0.0156
SCFXM1	0.9360	0.1716	0.671	0.1076	0.8369	0.1211	1.5756	0.9204	0.7956	0.1560	0.7956	0.1716
SCFXM2	7.0356	1.482	4.6819	0.8760	5.1343	1.0299	13.7281	8.7985	6.2556	1.3416	6.5052	1.716
SCFXM3	25.8338	7.6440	18.7696	3.0041	19.1410	3.2197	54.9748	38.5478	21.4813	5.2260	23.1661	6.9576
SCORPION	0.7488	0.0624	0.5746	0.0396	0.7092	0.0455	0.9360	0.2340	0.7644	0.0624	0.7332	0.0780
SCRS8	6.4740	1.1856	4.8940	0.4658	5.0458	0.5091	9.8281	5.3664	5.2416	0.8112	5.3040	0.9048
SCTAP1	0.1716	0.0780	0.1251	0.0341	0.1374	0.0390	0.4680	0.3744	0.1716	0.1248	0.1872	0.0624
SCTAP3	3.7752	2.2776	1.7438	1.0635	1.8615	1.1210	104.7391	103.5223	7.0356	5.9124	7.2072	6.2088
SHARE1B	0.2340	0.0312	0.2096	0.0155	0.2195	0.0181	0.3120	0.1560	0.1872	0.0156	0.1560	0.0468
SHARE2B	0.0624	0.0241	0.0339	0.0158	0.0464	0.0178	0.0468	0.0468	0.0312	0.0212	0.0312	0.0212
SHIP04L	5.8812	0.0936	5.5653	0.0465	5.7380	0.0510	5.4600	0.0312	5.4444	0.0156	5.4756	0.0468
SHIP04S	2.2308	0.0156	1.9913	0.0070	2.1237	0.0084	1.9188	0.0312	1.9188	0.0312	1.9032	0.0312
SHIP08L	25.163	0.2340	24.0501	0.0932	24.4794	0.1004	26.177	2.5896	23.8214	0.2340	23.9462	0.2964
SHIP08S	4.2432	0.1092	4.0686	0.0410	4.1066	0.0436	4.3680	0.5304	3.8688	0.0780	3.8688	0.0936
SHIP12L	55.3648	0.1716	55.0681	0.0787	55.2934	0.0852	59.1244	5.6628	53.8359	0.3588	53.9763	0.3588
SHIP12S	7.6440	0.0936	7.5187	0.0334	7.6120	0.0357	8.4709	1.4196	7.1292	0.0780	7.1448	0.0624
STOCFOR1	0.0468	0.0250	0.4180	0.0101	0.4271	0.0114	0.0624	0.0156	0.0468	0.0030	0.0312	0.005
Average	4.5846	0.5348	4.0231	0.2516	4.1244	0.2761	9.3803	5.6185	4.3286	0.5718	4.4172	0.6680

validation and verification phase follows, so, the decision maker may upload the input data to the DSS and select the algorithms and the basis update methods to be evaluated, in the next step. Then, the algorithms evaluation and execution step follows. The last step includes the presentation and the analysis of the results. Finally, the decision maker validates the results and if necessary provides feedback on the operation and the updated decision making process is performed again.

The sequence diagram in Figure 3 shows the whole interaction between the decision maker and the DSS in order to produce the report that will assist further in the decision making process. The decision-policy maker interacts with the initial screen of the DSS and uploads the input file, selects the algorithms (RSM and\or EPSA) and basis update methods (full inverse and\or PFI and\or MPFI) and presses the 'Report' button. Then, the system validates the input data and executes the RSM and EPSA algorithms for each basis update method, collects the total execution time, the time to perform the basis inverse, the number of iterations and the objective value, and presents these results in the report screen. Finally, the decision maker can export the results as a pdf file.

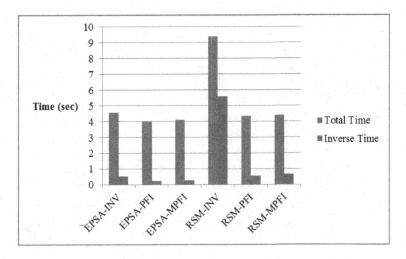

Fig. 1. Average Total and Inverse Time of the Exterior and Revised Simplex Algorithm Using Three Different Updating Methods over the Netlib Set

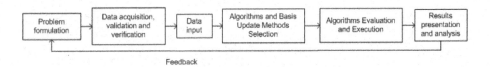

Fig. 2. Decision Making Process

Figure 4 presents the class diagram of the DSS. InitialScreen is a boundary class that includes three methods responding to decision maker's action events: i) upload input file, ii) select algorithms and basis update methods, and iii) press 'Report' button. SimplexAlgorithm is an abstract class that incorporates the common attributes and methods of RevisedSimplexAlgorithm and Exterior-PrimalSimplexAlgorithm. Matrix A contains the constraints coefficients, vector c the objective function coefficients, vector b the right-hand side values, vector Eqin the type of constraints (equality or inequality), and variable minMax the type of problem (minimization or maximization). Moreover, the SimplexAlgorithm class includes three methods that perform the basis update methods and an abstract method for the execution of the algorithms' logic. Finally, the RevisedSimplexAlgorithm and ExteriorPrimalSimplexAlgorithm classes override the abstract method executeAlgorithm of the SimplexAlgorithm and perform their steps for the solution of the linear programming problem.

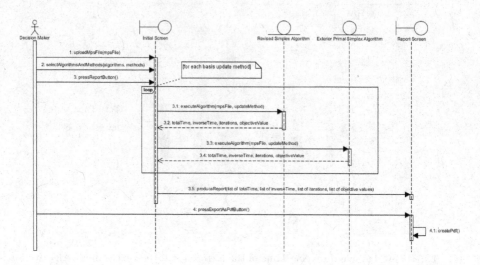

Fig. 3. Sequence Diagram

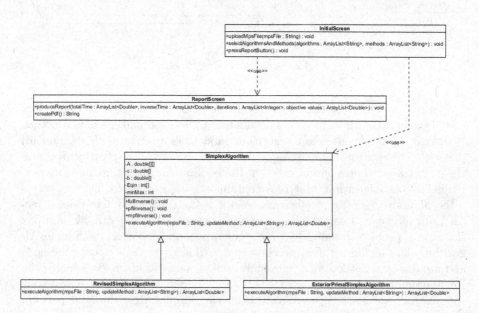

Fig. 4. Class Diagram

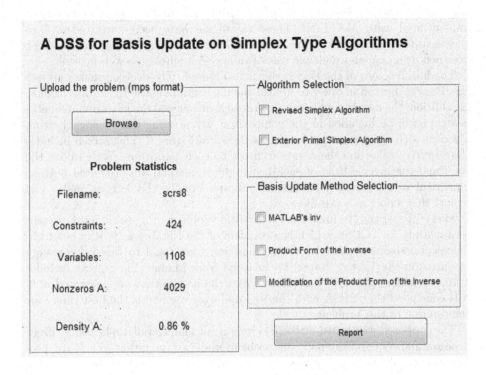

Fig. 5. Initial Screen of the web-based DSS

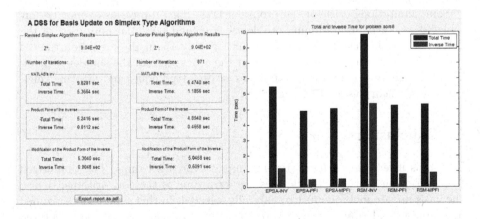

Fig. 6. Report of the Results

5.2   DSS Presentation

As stated in the previous section, all algorithms and update methods have been implemented using MATLAB. These algorithms have been converted to Java classes using the MATLAB Builder JA. The web interface of the DSS has been designed using jsp and multiple users can access it through a web browser.

The initial screen of the DSS is shown in Figure 5. The decision maker presses the 'Browse' button in order to upload the file containing the LP in mps format. In addition, the decision maker selects the algorithms and the basis update methods that will be included in the comparison. By pressing the 'Report' button, a screen with a report is presented, as shown in Figure 6. This screen includes the objective value and the iterations made by each algorithm. Furthermore, the total and the inverse time of each basis update method are presented both as numerical values and in an illustrative figure. Finally, the decision maker can export this report as a pdf file.

Many LPs of the Netlib set are real-world problems. Figures 5 and 6 present a case study for SCRS8, which is a problem of the Netlib set. SCRS8 is a technological assessment model for the transition from fossil to renewable energy resources in the United States [11] adapted from Manne [15]. SCRS8 includes 1,169 variables with 491 constraints. From the results that are presented in 6, it is concluded that EPSA with the PFI updating method is the best choice for the solution of this problem.

The proposed web-based DSS offers important managerial implications. First, decision makers can formulate the problem under examination as a linear programming problem and get a thorough analysis. Problems that can be formulated as linear programming problems include telecommunications, bio-informatics, supply chain management, etc. Moreover, the decision-policy maker gets an overview of the type of the algorithm and basis update method that best suits to a specific problem.

Some limitations exist on the proposed DSS. Some problems cannot be formulated as linear programming problems. A second potential limitation of the proposed DSS is that it provides information only about the execution time of the basis update step; information about the other steps of the simplex type algorithms, like preconditioning techniques, scaling techniques and pivoting rules, can also be incorporated to the DSS.

6   Conclusions

The basis inverse is a crucial step in simplex-type algorithms. The time taken to perform the basis inverse dictates the total time of these algorithms. Hence, the basis update method must be carefully selected. In this paper, we performed a computational comparison of three basis update methods and incorporated them on EPSA and RSM. The results showed that PFI scheme is faster than MATLAB's inv and MPFI. Furthermore, the percentage of the time to compute the basis inverse to the total time is bigger in the RSM than EPSA.

However, there are some instances that MPFI scheme is faster than PFI and the basis inverse time is bigger in EPSA than RSM. So, there isn't any best algorithm or best method for all instances. We have implemented a web-based DSS in order to assist decision-policy makers in the selection of the algorithm and basis update method to solve their LPs. All algorithms have been implemented using MATLAB and converted to Java classes using the MATLAB Builder JA. The web interface of the DSS has been designed using jsp and users can access it through a web browser from their PC/laptop or their smart device.

In future work, we plan to enhance the DSS with other options that will give decision maker the opportunity to control all the steps of simplex type algorithms. More specifically, we plan to add preconditioning techniques, scaling techniques and pivoting rules. Finally, we plan to present real application case studies that the proposed DSS can be utilized.

References

1. Bartels, R.H., Golub, G.H.: The Simplex Method of Linear Programming Using LU Decomposition. Communications of the ACM 12, 266–268 (1969)
2. Bhargava, H.K., Krishnan, R.: The World Wide Web: opportunities for operations research and management science. INFORMS Journal on Computing 10, 359–383 (1998)
3. Bhargava, H.K., Power, D.J., Sun, D.: Progress in Web-based decision support technologies. Decision Support Systems 43(4), 1083–1095 (2007)
4. Benhamadou, M.: On the Simplex Algorithm 'Revised Form'. Advances in Engineering Software 33, 769–777 (2002)
5. Dantzig, G.B.: Computational Algorithm of the Revised Simplex Method. RAND Report RM-1266. The RAND Corporation, Santa Monica, CA (1953)
6. Dantzig, G.B., Orchard-Hays, M.: The Product Form of the Inverse in the Simplex Method. Math. Comp. 8, 64–67 (1954)
7. Forrest, J.H., Tomlin, J.A.: Updated Triangular Factors of the Basis to Maintain Sparsity in the Product form Simplex Method. Mathematical Programming 2, 263–278 (1972)
8. Gay, D.M.: Electronic Mail Distribution of Linear Programming Test Problems. Mathematical Programming Society COAL Newsletter 13, 10–12 (1985)
9. Ghodsypour, S.H., O'Brien, C.: A decision support system for supplier selection using an integrated analytic hierarchy process and linear programming. International Journal of Production Economics 56, 199–212 (1998)
10. Hernández, J.E., Zarate, P., Dargam, F., Delibašić, B., Liu, S., Ribeiro, R. (eds.): EWG-DSS 2011. LNBIP, vol. 121. Springer, Heidelberg (2012)
11. Ho, J.K.: Nested decomposition of a dynamic energy model. Management Science 23, 1022–1026 (1977)
12. Lappi, J., Nuutinen, T., Siitonen, M.: A linear programming software for multilevel forest management planning. In: Management Systems for a Global Economy with Global Resource Concerns, pp. 470–482 (1996)
13. Lauer, J., Jacobs, L.W., Brusco, M.J., Bechtold, S.E.: An interactive, optimization-based decision support system for scheduling part-time, computer lab attendants. Omega 22(6), 613–626 (1994)

14. Lourenço, J.C., Morton, A., Bana e Costa, C.A.: PROBE-A multicriteria decision support system for portfolio robustness evaluation. Decision Support Systems 54, 534–550 (2012)
15. Manne, A.S.: Sufficient conditions for optimality in an infinite horizon development plan. Econometrica 38, 18–38 (1970)
16. Markowitz, H.: The Elimination Form of the Inverse and its Applications to Linear Programming. Management Science 3, 255–269 (1957)
17. Ordóñez, F., Freund, R.: Computational experience and the explanatory value of condition measures for linear optimization. SIAM J. Optimization 14(2), 307–333 (2003)
18. Paparrizos, K., Samaras, N., Stephanides, G.: An Efficient Simplex Type Algorithm for Sparse and Dense Linear Programs. European Journal of Operational Research 148(2), 323–334 (2003)
19. Ploskas, N., Samaras, N.: A Computational Comparison of Basis Updating Schemes for the Simplex Algorithm on a CPU-GPU System. Journal of Computational Science (2013); Paper under review
20. Power, D.J., Kaparthi, S.: Building Web-based decision support systems. Studies in Informatics and Control 11(4), 291–302 (2002)
21. Reid, J.: A Sparsity-exploiting Variant of the Bartels-Golub Decomposition for Linear Programming Base. Mathematical Programming 24, 55–69 (1982)
22. Suhl, L.M., Suhl, U.H.: A Fast LU Update for Linear Programming. Annals of Operations Research 43(1), 33–47 (1993)
23. Venkataramanan, M.A., Bornstein, M.: A decision support system for parking space assignment. Mathematical and Computer Modelling 15(8), 71–76 (1991)

Decision Analysis in Magnox Limited: Developments in Techniques and Stakeholder Engagement Processes

Simon Turner and Stephen Wilmott

Magnox Limited, Berkeley, Gloucestershire
simon.d.turner@magnoxsites.com
http://www.magnoxsites.co.uk/

Abstract. This paper outlines the legislative requirements for optimisation of radioactive wastes and provides a brief background to the history of the use of . Multi-Attribute Decision Analysis (MADA) optioneering tools in Magnox Limited for the purposes of waste management decision-making and stakeholder engagement. The paper then outlines the challenges that traditional optioneering approaches presented Magnox as the Company moved towards decommissioning its fleet of nuclear power stations, and then describes the new assessment techniques that the authors developed in response to this challenge providing an open, transparent and proportionate approach to decision-making and periodic review of the decisions taken.

Keywords: Multi-Attribute Decision Analysis, Nuclear Decommissioning, BPEO Screening Analysis, Stakeholder Engagement, Periodic Review.

1   Introduction

This paper is not presented as a traditional research paper, but instead presents how the authors have developed an alternative decision analysis process as a solution to the difficulties presented by existing methodologies in demonstrating the optimisation of radioactive wastes in the nuclear industry. Thus it is acknowledged by the authors that the paper is not presented in the context of existing research in decision support systems, but instead describes an alternative approach that may be of interest to the academic community, that has been applied to a specific industry to address a specific problem.

The paper presents the requirement for optimisation within the nuclear industry, why a new approach to decision making was required by clearly describing the weaknesses in traditional Multi-Attribute Decision Analysis (MADA) approaches, and then describes the new approach and how it is being applied.

This work is already benefitting Magnox, and the value of the decision process is validated with feedback from the Environment Agency. Other nuclear operators in the UK are also already benefitting from this work, and this work will gain further importance as more existing generating stations start to enter into the decommissioning phase of their lifecycles.

Further, the authors consider that application of these techniques could help other industries dealing with large numbers of multiple decision assessments.

J.E. Hernández et al. (Eds.): EWG-DSS 2012, LNBIP 164, pp. 115–125, 2013.

2 Optimisation of Radioactive Waste Management in the Nuclear Industry in the UK

2.1 Requirements for Optimisation

Following the end of electricity generation, the decommissioning of nuclear plant will involve dealing with a variety of radioactive wastes, determined by various thresholds – Intermediate Level Waste (ILW), Low Level Waste (LLW) and Very Low Level Waste (VLLW). There is a requirement on the industry to ensure that its waste management plans are optimised at strategic and detailed levels. Under previous regulatory requirements the former was undertaken by high-level optioneering within a framework called Best Practicable Environmental Option (BPEO), and the latter within a framework called Best Practicable Means (BPM).[1, 2]

BPEO is usually defined as [Ref. 2],

> "...the outcome of a systematic and consultative decision-making procedure which emphasises the protection and conservation of the environment across air, land and water. The BPEO procedure establishes for a given set of objectives, the option that provides the most benefit or least damage to the environment as a whole, at acceptable cost, in the long term as in the short term".

BPM can be defined as [Ref. 3],

> "Within a particular waste management option, the BPM is that...level of management and engineering control that minimises, as far as is practicable, the release of radioactivity to the environment whilst taking into account a wider range of factors, including cost effectiveness, technological status, operational safety and societal factors..."

2.2 History of Decision Making in Magnox Limited

Prior to the Aarhus Convention (1998) and the European Council Directive on Public Access to Environmental Information (2003)[3], regarding access to information and encouraging greater stakeholder participation in the decision making processes on matters concerning the environment, there was some use of decision analysis techniques in the company but little evidence of them being used as a means of stakeholder engagement [for example, Ref. 4]. However, with the introduction of these requirements, the company recognised the need for greater openness and

---

[1] In England and Wales, introduction of the Environmental Permitting Regulations 2010 has replaced these terms with Best Available Techniques (BAT), although both BPEO and BPM processes continue to be used, and are acknowledged by regulators as useful steps in determination of BAT by identifying high level strategy and implementation optimisation respectively.

[2] Additional information on the requirements for optimisation may be found in the Nuclear Industry Code of Practice [Ref. 1].

[3] This was introduced in the UK through the Environmental Information Regulations (2004).

transparency in its decision-making processes, and with MADA assessment tools already being practised in some arenas, and being available in "simple-to-use" off the shelf packages such as "HiView", it soon became clear that such tools could be used as the means for engagement.

For demonstration primarily of BPEO for decisions relating to waste management for ILW and LLW wastes, so workshops began to be held with representation from a variety of stakeholder interests (including Site Stakeholder Groups (SSG), regulators and non-governmental organisations) to assess alternative options to support development of strategy for each waste. A simple process was used, illustrated in Figure 1, with individual sites identifying wastes, compiling lists of options, assessing them through MADA techniques and then reporting on outcomes.

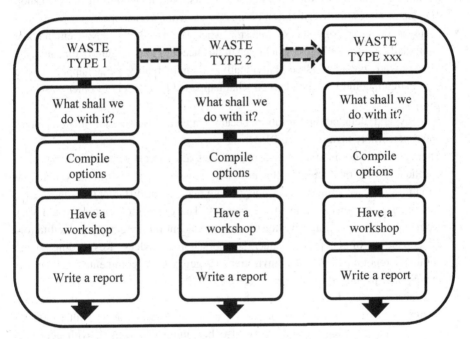

Fig. 1. The Standard Process of Decision-Making (and Stakeholder Engagement) for Individual Waste Streams

3   The Need for Change

However, the change to a more stakeholder led decision making process resulted in a number of problems:

- Magnox Ltd has some 500 different radioactive waste types, identified by location and characteristics. In principle each of these wastes could require their own BPEO assessment [Ref. 5].

- The MADA assessments were often carried out by external organisations that were not well practised in understanding the theory behind the available software packages: for example, weighting factors were being averaged, or the differences between swing and preference weighting were misunderstood.
- Reports would often contain many figures showing weighted scores and sensitivity analyses, but with little underpinned justification for outcomes.
- Sensitivity analysis became restricted to effects of weighting factors on attribute scores.
- The process was resource intensive. Workshops and associated work cost the organisation between £10,000 and £2 million, with typical costs around £15-20,000 – in addition to this would be staff costs, both in support of the workshop but also in review and verification of the outputs from workshops.
- Changes in technology, in an industry where technological advancements are continually made, could result in large studies needing to be regularly repeated.
- Wastes were being assessed individually, when in reality what happened to a waste stream could be dependent on what happened to a variety of other wastes on site.
- Strategy and detailed optimisation became intertwined, so that small changes could potentially invalidate the BPEO.
- There was no coordination between outcomes at different sites, so often reports conflicted with one another for no good reason (recognising individual site variations may sometimes result in legitimate reasons for different outcomes).
- Regulators were losing faith in the process. The outputs of reports would vary from site to site for similar waste streams, dependent on the quality of facilitation, understanding of the process, and the workshop attendees. Responding to the summary reports of 2005, the Environment Agency (EA) commented, "*there was much paper produced...with little evidence of it being useful to either party.*"
- The process was disengaging stakeholders who were fatigued by the process, leading to dwindling numbers of participants, hence reducing the value input of the engagement. Magnox staff were also becoming disengaged, with decisions seemingly being stakeholder led rather than by those considered to have expertise in such arenas; for example, one study was scored and weighted solely by non-expert members of the public.

It was clear that simply applying MADAs to every decision on waste management strategy, notwithstanding the high cost of doing so, was not an effective way forward, either in terms of delivering well underpinned decision making or engagement with stakeholders. Further, to continue using the existing process would have potentially resulted in significant delays to the whole decommissioning process.

4   Development of a New Process of Decision Analysis

To address these issues, the authors developed a four step process of decision analysis (Figure 2) [Ref. 6]:

a. Establish a site waste baseline strategy by application of the MADA approach (this was undertaken for ILW only, as a site baseline for LLW does not make operational sense). Stakeholders were involved in the process to assign attribute weightings, recognising that different people have different views as to the relative importance of the various issues involved.
b. For each waste, a screening matrix is used to identify the availability of other technical options.
c. The available options are then compared to the site baseline to consider whether such options would deliver improvements in terms of waste disposal volume or management solution along the waste hierarchy.
d. Review the BPEOs on a periodic basis.

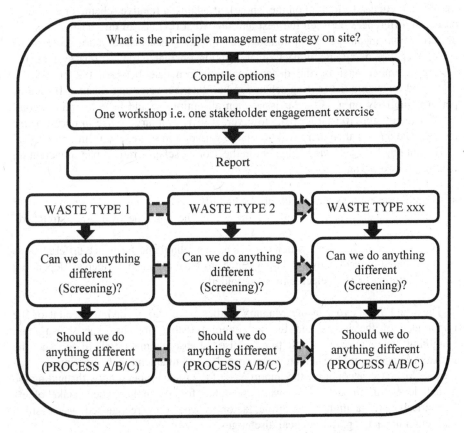

Fig. 2. The New Process of Decision Making Based on Establishing a Site Baseline and Screening Analysis

4.1   Establishing the Site Baseline Strategy – The "Meaning of Ten" Approach to MADA

For the site baseline studies, options providing the widest contrast in concept were considered in order to understand the underlying drivers [for example, Ref. 7]. That said, a wide range of options did not necessarily result in a large number of options as the number of widely applicable, appropriate technologies are relatively limited – the site baseline is therefore not especially sensitive to technology change.

An approach we call the "Meaning of Ten Approach" was developed and used, with attributes largely related to impacts (e.g. tonnes of carbon dioxide emitted) rather than the mechanisms which give rise to impacts (e.g. transport). This allowed for clarity of reasoning when assigning weighting factors to attributes and also facilitated subsequent sensitivity analysis (e.g. because a new mechanism resulting in carbon dioxide emissions, for example, can be later included in the analysis if required). The authors also believed that this helped external stakeholders understand the magnitude of the actual consequences of adopting particular strategies.

In the Magnox site baseline strategy studies, an absolute scoring scheme was used (based on factual information on the whole), as against a relative scheme or a scheme based on differences between the best and the worst options. In this scheme, a score of zero would mean that an option had "no impact" on an issue and a score of 10 represented the maximum impact of any option on that issue. In this system, the "swing" element, that is, the difference in performance between the options, is accounted for within the scoring scheme rather than the weighting scheme. If options perform similarly on a particular issue then all options would have a similar score, e.g. between 9 and 10 (out of 10). However, if there is a large range in performance between the options then there will be a large variation in score, e.g. from 1 to 10.

Accounting for the "swing" element in the scoring scheme rather than in weighting factors has two advantages:

a. It minimises the risk that small, unreliable differences in option performance could (mathematically) have an undue influence in the outcome by being "stretched" between scores of zero and 10; and,
b. It allows for attributes on which options have a reliable performance difference (as represented by scores over a larger range) to have a greater influence, depending on weighting factors selected by stakeholders.

The weighting factors in the Magnox studies were chosen taking account of the importance of the issues and the maximum possible impacts. The scoring and weighting system allowed people to recognise the absolute magnitude of an issue (the worst an impact could be, i.e. the meaning of 10) and to amend the weighting factor if they so wished to account for the importance of the issue to them, notwithstanding the actual level of impact. This was apparent, for example, when stakeholders consciously gave a higher weighting factor to what they recognised was a small maximum impact, e.g. radiological discharges.

In these ways, the scoring and weighting process took into account differences in option performance, the absolute levels of impact concerned, the potential for error due to uncertainties, and subjective preferences in terms of importance of the issues notwithstanding actual impacts. The process also allowed for analysis of alternative scenarios, given the parameters and constraints identified by stakeholder views of potential impacts.

4.2   Consideration of Individual Waste Streams

With the site baseline established, the screening process is applied [for example, Ref. 8], using a matrix approach, and involving waste management experts from the Company and the individual sites. This process compares at a high level, for each waste stream at each site, the site baseline option against other management technologies to identify the availability of technical solutions (a process which took a 1-day workshop for 39 waste streams at Hinkley Point A site with no need for external facilitation). Technologies are assessed to determine whether they deliver improvements in opportunities along the waste hierarchy, or if requiring disposal, substantial reductions in the waste volume to be disposed, from that identified by the baseline option. A simple triage approach can then be applied to the outcome of the process for the purpose of options comparison (see Figure 3):

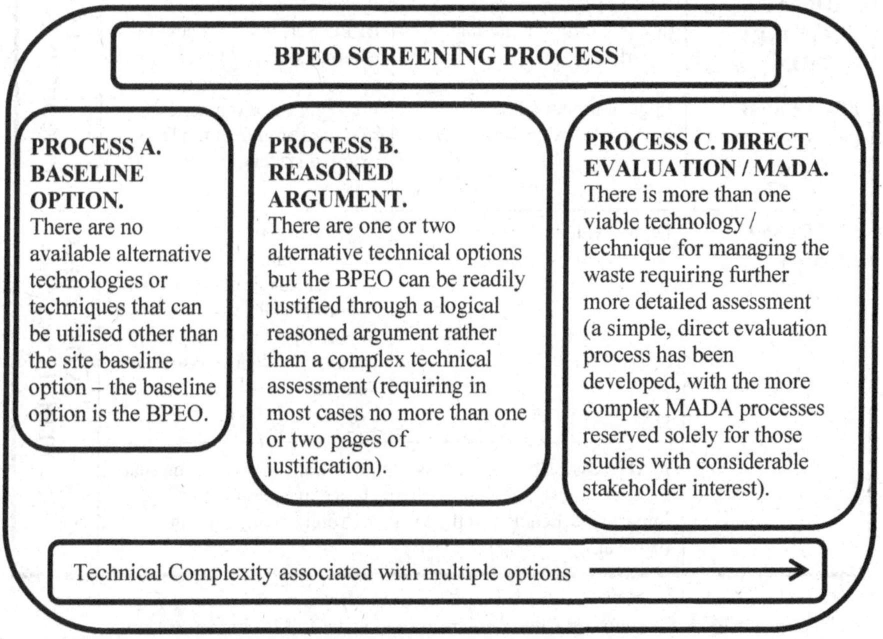

BPEO SCREENING PROCESS

PROCESS A. BASELINE OPTION.
There are no available alternative technologies or techniques that can be utilised other than the site baseline option – the baseline option is the BPEO.

PROCESS B. REASONED ARGUMENT.
There are one or two alternative technical options but the BPEO can be readily justified through a logical reasoned argument rather than a complex technical assessment (requiring in most cases no more than one or two pages of justification).

PROCESS C. DIRECT EVALUATION / MADA.
There is more than one viable technology / technique for managing the waste requiring further more detailed assessment (a simple, direct evaluation process has been developed, with the more complex MADA processes reserved solely for those studies with considerable stakeholder interest).

Technical Complexity associated with multiple options $\longrightarrow$

Fig. 3. Post Screening Outcomes for Options Comparison.

In other words, the process employs a proportionate approach to decision making and identification of the BPEO. Experience thus far has demonstrated that over 99% of the waste streams evaluated can be dealt with using either Process A or B, presenting a considerable cost and time saving to the Company.

5   Stakeholder Involvement in the New Process

The approach to stakeholder involvement has also been given consideration and a proportionate approach to involvement and engagement developed. The principle of participation does not necessarily mean that all potential stakeholders need to be involved in every BPEO study. Instead stakeholders input into the "big picture" for the site, but in general do not need to be involved with the detail of hundreds of individual waste streams (Figure 4).

	INTERNAL	EXTERNAL	
BPEO SCREENING PROCESS	Involvement of technical specialists with knowledge of the waste streams and possible technical solutions.	External stakeholders briefed with outcome of screening process.	*EXTERNAL STAKEHOLDER ENGAGEMENT*
PROCESS A BASELINE OPTION	Baseline option further justified through internal expertise.	Presentation of outcome of BPEO Screening Process to external stakeholders.	
PROCESS B REASONED ARGUMENT	Logical argument developed by internal expertise.	Presentation of outcome of reasoned argument made to external stakeholders.	
PROCESS C DIRECT EVALUATION / MADA	Direct evaluation process undertaken by internal expertise to compare options. *OR*	Presentation of outcome of direct evaluation made to external stakeholders but with opportunity for stakeholders to participate in a weighting exercise to identify issues of concern. *OR*	*EXTERNAL STAKEHOLDER INVOLVEMENT*
	MADA assessment held to compare options involving internal and external stakeholders, where choice of option is likely to impact significantly on the local environment, e.g. on-site disposal.		

Fig. 4. Stakeholder Engagement in the Decision Making Process

6   Periodic Review of BPEOs

The developed process has also recognised the need for ensuring that the outputs of these assessments are updated regularly to reflect changes in waste characterisation and analysis, or new technologies, or even changes in regulation and timescales for decommissioning.

The success of this process is that a simple review of the screening process means that individual screening forms can be reviewed quickly and usually simply revalidated rather than necessarily reconvening workshops to determine the MADA output for each and every waste stream that is affected.

All of the BPEO documentation is kept on a database which links all documents to individual waste stream identifiers for all sites, and employs a simple "traffic-light system" to raise awareness that a periodic review is required.

The outcome of the review can then be recorded on the BPEO Requirements Form [Ref. 6] and also recorded on the database. In other words, the whole process from start to end is fully transparent and auditable, with each step clearly documented along the way.

7   Comments and Feedback

The BPEO Screening Process and the BPEO Database have been introduced to the Environment Agency Inspection Team and both have been well received. The Environment Agency has commented [Ref. 9],

> *"We always welcome developments that make our job as well as the sites' easier and more efficient. We are able to check rapidly if a site has the structure in place to demonstrate compliance in this area and it reassures us that best practice is being applied...Over the coming years it will be critical in ensuring wastes go to the right disposal route allowing decommissioning that gives optimised protection of the environment."*

Magnox Site experience of the process has also been very favourable, with interest generated now amongst other nuclear operators in the UK [Ref. 10]:

> *"Prior to the implementation of the new BPEO methodology, the process would typically involve several months of effort and costs to deliver an outcome. The new methodology is much more efficient and less times consuming, and also allows comparison with similar wastes at other sites which allows a generic approach to be taken to managing our wastes."*
>
> Head of Environment, Hinkley Point A

> *"Having employed this novel process at the recent Hinkley Point A Site ILW BPEO Workshop, it is clear that this technique facilitates decision making by presenting information in a clear, tabular format that can be easily understood and discussed by panel members (including non-experts)."*
>
> Head of Waste, Hinkley Point A

"At Berkeley we are undertaking BPEO reviews for over 100 different ILW streams that need to be retrieved and made safe prior to entry into care and maintenance. With previous approaches this would have required generation of lots of supporting information for each waste stream and each option to support MADA workshops. With the revised approach...this will result in both a significant cost and time saving, whilst still maintaining regulator and stakeholder engagement and support for a robust process and outcome."

Berkeley ILW Project Design Authority

"The development of the BPEO Screening Process and BPEO Database has produced a process that is already attracting interest from other Site Licence Companies (SLCs). By simplifying the process it allows all those involved to think more about the outcome than being immersed in the process. This should improve the outcome and involvement in the process."

Magnox South Head of Environment.

The development of this approach and its practical application has also been recognised by the Operational Research Society, where it was a finalist for the prestigious President's Medal in 2012, and has also won awards from IdeasUK (Public Sector, 2011) and the Nuclear Decommissioning Authority (2011).

8   Conclusion

Fundamentally without redevelopment of the optioneering process, decommissioning projects in Magnox Limited would have ground to a halt – we could not have continued to operate as a business whilst fulfilling our legal requirements. Thus far, 190 waste streams have now been addressed in two years of operating the process, across ten decommissioning nuclear power stations.

The development of this new and innovative approach to BPEO management across Magnox Limited provides a much improved level of consistency, efficiency and transparency delivering better integrated, holistic outcomes. The process has also opened the way for a more open, transparent and proportionate approach to BPEO regulation with the Environmental Agencies, which has been welcomed on all sides, and also involves stakeholders when it is important to do so – when what is under consideration can impact them.

Finally, this has had, and will continue to have, enormous savings (running into millions of pounds) in terms of both time and ongoing costs for the organisation as we move forward, through both the application of a proportionate approach to optioneering assessment, and also the opportunities identified for consolidated waste management approaches.

The authors consider that the lessons learnt in development of this approach, and the approach itself may present a useful contribution to other nuclear operators, particularly as they enter decommissioning (indeed a lot of interest has already been generated within the nuclear sector in the UK).

It is recognised that this approach was developed to resolve the particular optimisation problem that faced Magnox. However, it is considered that the approach may contribute to the decision-making and decision support environment in other industries outside of the nuclear sector where multiple decisions are required, over a short duration (at multiple sites) but in a clear, transparent and auditable manner. Further work would be required to develop the process for this purpose.

References

1. Nuclear Industry Safety Directors Forum. Best Available Techniques for the Management of the Generation and Disposal of Radioactive Wastes – A Nuclear Industry Code of Practice (December 2010)
2. Royal Commission on Environmental Pollution (1976)
3. Department of Environment. Cm2919 Review of Radioactive Waste Management Policy: Final Conclusions (1995)
4. Phillips, A., Skennerton, S.K.: Assessment of the Best Practicable Environmental Option (BPEO) for the Management of Hunterston A Operational Intermediate Level Radioactive Wastes (August 1993)
5. Nuclear Decommissioning Authority UK Radioactive Waste Inventory (2010), http://www.nda.gov.uk/ukinventory/
6. Magnox Standard S-391. Procedures for the Production of Best Practicable Environmental Option (BPEO) Studies (2011)
7. Turner, S., et al.: Option Study for the Long Term Management of Operational ILW at Berkeley Site (October 2010)
8. Turner, S.: Screening Form for ILW Sludge (9G16/ 9G17) at Trawsfynydd (May 2012)
9. Email correspondence from the Environment Agency to S. Turner (January 2011)
10. Turner, S.: Presentation to NEDCON 2012. BAT Assessment in Practice. Intermediate Level Waste (ILW) Management in Magnox (April 2012)

Author Index